DATE			

THIS
ISN'T
GOING
TO END
WELL

ALSO BY DANIEL WALLACE

Big Fish

Ray in Reverse

The Watermelon King

Mr. Sebastian and the Negro Magician

The Kings and Queens of Roam

Extraordinary Adventures

The Cat's Pajamas

THIS ISN'T GOING TO END WELL

The True Story of a Man I Thought I Knew

BY

Daniel Wallace

ILLUSTRATIONS BY

William Nealy

ALGONQUIN BOOKS OF CHAPEL HILL 2023

Published by
Algonquin Books of Chapel Hill
Post Office Box 2225
Chapel Hill, North Carolina 27515-2225

an imprint of Workman Publishing Co., Inc.,
a subsidiary of Hachette Book Group, Inc.
1290 Avenue of the Americas
New York, New York 10104

Printed in the United States of America.
Design by Steve Godwin.

The publisher is not responsible for websites (or their content) that are not owned
by the publisher.

I've quoted portions of "Mr. December" by David Madison (*The Independent*,
April 17, 2002) with permission of the author. All of William Nealy's maps and
published illustrations are reproduced by the kind permission of Adventure Keen
Communications. All quotes used by permission. To purchase books and maps
by William Nealy, please visit adventurewithkeen.com.

Library of Congress Cataloging-in-Publication Data
Names: Wallace, Daniel, 1959– author. | Nealy, William, 1953–2001, illustrator.
Title: This isn't going to end well : the true story of a man I thought I knew /
by Daniel Wallace ; illustrations by William Nealy. Other titles: This is not going
to end well
Description: Chapel Hill, North Carolina : Algonquin Books of Chapel Hill, 2023.
| Summary: "The author tries to come to terms with the life and death of his
multitalented longtime friend and brother-in-law, who had been his biggest hero
and inspiration"—Provided by publisher.
Identifiers: LCCN 2022048015 | ISBN 9781643752105 (hardcover) |
ISBN 9781643753720 (ebook)
Subjects: LCSH: Wallace, Daniel, 1959—Friends and associates. | Nealy, William,
1953–2001. | Authors, American—20th century—Biography. | Illustrators—
United States—Biography. | LCGFT: Autobiographies.
Classification: LCC PS3573.A4256348 Z46 2023 | DDC 813/.54 [B]—
dc23/eng/20221014
LC record available at https://lccn.loc.gov/2022048015

10 9 8 7 6 5 4 3 2 1
First Edition

In memory of Randall Garrett Kenan

AUTHOR'S NOTE

This is a book about the life and death of William Nealy, my brother-in-law, a man I loved and admired and who left this world, by choice, when he was forty-eight years old. He was so young, and now that I have outlived him by a decade and a half, he seems even younger. This is fitting: William had the worldview of an adventurous teenager all his life, incorporating those passions into his adult self: drawing cartoons, climbing mountains, kayaking rivers, hunting for fossils on the banks of the Eno River, keeping snakes as pets, making books. I thought he'd been living the kind of life he wanted to. Then he killed himself. That day— July 19, 2001—marks the before and after of my family's life.

Suicide is one of the most traumatic of deaths, no matter how it's undertaken, and those left behind suffer through a complicated grief that may never subside. That grief in my life, enduring for the last twenty-two years, was the true impetus for this book. I didn't begin it with the idea that writing it would be cathartic, or that I would "come to terms" with his suicide (I don't even know what that would mean, in this case). But I did want to try to understand him and tell his story the best I could. I have tried to recreate events, locales, and conversations from my memories of them. To protect privacy, in some instances I have changed the names of individuals and places. But none of the changes undermine the essence of William's story in any way.

Though William's reasons for dying by suicide were uniquely his own, the choice he made is all too common. There are resources to help. The National Suicide Prevention Lifeline number is (800) 273-8255. There is also a three-digit dialing code—988—that will route callers directly to the Lifeline. You can also text 741741 to be connected with a trained counselor, twenty-four hours a day.

One of the major challenges in preventing suicide is that thoughts of it are often kept secret until it's too late. It's one of the most powerful and damaging secrets a person can have, too, and only becomes more insidious the longer it's kept. So please, tell us your secrets. Show us who you are.

—Daniel Wallace

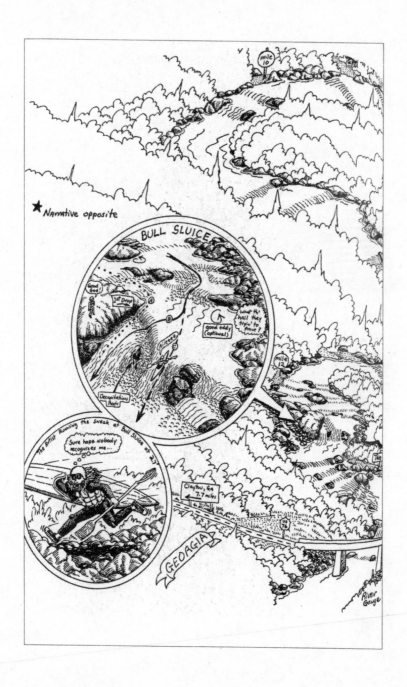

★ Narrative opposite

THIS
ISN'T
GOING
TO END
WELL

Part One

THE FIRST TIME I saw him he was standing on the roof of our house, wearing frayed and faded cutoffs and nothing else, eyeing the swimming pool about twenty-five feet below. *William*. Last name unknown, unnecessary. Already—in my mind, at least—he had achieved the single-name status of a rock star, and I had yet to even meet him. I'd only heard about him from Holly, my sister, who was older than me by six years. My sister's boyfriend was on the roof.

It was unclear why he was there at first, though he did have the look of someone about to take a leap. But that was impossible: the pool was on the ground, and he was on the roof of our house. Out of utmost concern for any potential accidents, my mother had had the diving board removed, and that had been just three feet above the water. He was eight times higher than that. He had thick, corn-yellow hair tied back into a ponytail, broad shoulders, was thin at the waist, and he stood spotlighted by the sun. I thought, *Holy cow. He is about to jump.*

I was twelve. Until that day I never thought of a roof as a thing an actual person might, on purpose, jump off of. To get there, he'd first had to stand on the back porch railing, and then balance on a window sash, lift himself up and over the gutter, and roll away from the edge. After that it was a simple walk at a sloping forty-degree angle, barefoot on hot shingles, to the other side of the house, where the roof flattened out. This was the roof over my mother and father's bedroom, a 1960s addition to the 1930s house. He was standing at the edge of my parents' bedroom, surveying his flight path into the water.

My father did not like William at all.

He was definitely about to jump.

I guessed it could be done. It looked like it could be done. With a little lift he would miss the concrete skirt and splash into the deep end. But there were a multitude of ways for the jump to go wrong. He must have been considering a few of them. He could slip and miss the pool and hit the concrete instead. That was possible. But even if he hit the water, he couldn't know how fast and how deep his jump would carry him. He might hit bottom, break his legs, drown. He could crack his head. So many bad things could happen between the roof and the bottom of the pool.

Or maybe it wasn't William who was considering these things. Maybe it was just me.

And now he took the three steps back away from the edge of the roof for the running start, the bold approach, the liftoff. In my memory this happened in slow motion. Maybe it actually *was* in slow motion; maybe he was that good. And then he was airborne. *Freeze frame.*

It was toward the end of May. Summer had come to Birmingham, Alabama, hot for sure, but it wasn't the heat that knocked you back. It was the warm, wet blanket of humidity, the cottony air. But it was also beautifully green, and there were robins, cardinals, butterflies, and dragonflies everywhere, and the pool he was angling toward glittering and glinting like broken glass. A beautiful day to fly or, worse scenario, die. I was watching him through the back-door screen. Velma, our housekeeper, was upstairs ironing. He couldn't see me. I had just gotten home from school, seventh grade, my second year of private school. It was a boys' school, a former military academy, and everyone had to wear a tie and whenever an adult entered the room we had to stand, as if at attention. I was still wearing my tie. I was as thin and white as watered-down milk, and quiet, and I made straight Bs. I was okay at just about everything, the best at being average. And now this, this is what I was looking at, this man who was flying off our roof, falling through the air.

He hit the water, of course, made a giant splash, and disappeared beneath the wake, not for too long, but long enough for me to wonder if he would ever come up. Then he surfaced, leaning back his head to let the water pull his hair away from his face. Then he got out of the pool, climbed the house, and did it again. And again.

It was pretty magnificent. I was spellbound. It wasn't some unformed idea I had about masculinity or manliness in him that I was drawn to; I wasn't into that, then or now. It was just the wildness, the derring-do, his willingness to take flight—literally—into the unknown, an openness to experience and chance that so far in my short life had not been previously modeled to me by anyone. Whatever I was, it wasn't that, and I wasn't sure how much I wanted to be the me I was. That's what I would learn from him though, over the years, how to become the me I wanted. Not by being him, but by watching him.

Later though—much later—I wondered how the rest of our lives would have turned out had he died *that* day instead of the day he did, by his own hand, three decades later. Had he tried for the water but missed.

Holly would have lost her boyfriend of a year or so, and she would have carried that sorrow with her forever, how her first love had died *trying to dive into the pool from the roof of her parents' house.* Every man she'd be with for the rest of her life would eventually be told this story, every friend, and to some degree it would define her. But it would have been just *one* of the moments that defined her. She'd have gone on to other joys, other sorrows, fallen in love again and again and maybe even have had a family, maybe even have become, I don't know, a teacher. An artist. But as time passed, the day young William Nealy died trying to dive into our pool would dim. It would always be one of the most important days of her life, one of the worst, but in the end just another color in her quilt. And what would it have done to me? Who would I have become?

I didn't want him to die—on that day, watching him, or on any of the other days or nights he risked his life: kayaking a river above flood stage, falling off a mountain or a motorcycle, slamming his bike into a tree, drinking and driving, playing with venomous snakes. But his life was to have such a profound effect on Holly and me, and not all of it good. Sometimes I still imagine what it would have been like if he hadn't shared it with us after all.

But he did live. Some of William's friends came over later that day to join him. They laughed and whooped and hollered and jumped off the roof themselves and drank beer and smoked cigarettes, and my sister Holly, beautiful in her cutoff jeans and plain white T-shirt and long chocolate hair, laughed and drank with the rest of them. Holly, so bright and joyful and fearless. She was eighteen years old, three years out from the disease that would devour her. She jumped, too.

For a couple of hours, the house was like this, a circus of youth. Then it was over. I watched as they climbed off the roof, got in their beaters and drove away, and the house was quiet again, still.

William was so alive, more alive than I was or would ever be. He flew, and I, who couldn't, just watched. That someone so remarkable and dangerous could ever be reduced to ten cups of ashes in a small wooden box was unimaginable. That's what became of him, though, and it was in that box he came to stay with my wife and me, forty years after the first time I saw him. See him as I saw him that day, and then on all the days after, me the little brother of the beautiful sister, watching him hanging out in the kitchen in his leather jacket, a plain white T-shirt beneath it that matched

Holly's, his assassin-style sunglasses, his hair the color of burnt butter, thick, shoulder-length, straight, parted in the middle and sometimes falling across his face like a curtain; slender in his beaten-down jeans, the thick brown leather belt with grommets that held his jeans precariously right at his waist, a chain hooked on one end to a belt loop, the other end to his wallet, steel-toed black boots, leaning against the faux-slate kitchen counter where he'd set his black motorcycle helmet and not saying a word. Quiet. He seemed to be assembled from equal parts biker and builder, student and stud, and he pulled it off. At least I thought so, and that's all that mattered then, and it may be all that matters now. It was more than just a look, though: it was who he was beneath the disguise that made it work. It was who he was waiting to become. Sometimes you can tell.

He had been a cartoonist since he was a kid, an R. Crumb disciple; it wouldn't be long before I started seeing his drawings scattered around the house, taped to Holly's bedroom wall. "Cartoons became my second language," he later wrote. "Sometimes my first." His cartoons were funny, purposefully and playfully offensive, and popular with his friends. That he would go on to become a working artist and writer, a famous one at that, capturing the substance and style of a subculture and in the process becoming a subculture hero himself, surprised everybody, him most of all.

It was lucky for me to have met him when I did. He was the one who would give me the idea for the life I ended up living, even if what I ended up doing was nothing like him or what he did. He showed me how it was done: experience, imagine, then create. Every book I've written is dedicated to him in invisible ink. I doubt I would have written a one of them without him, or that I ever would have considered being an artist at all.

Who was he, though? In the mid-nineties a magazine editor asked him for his bio and William wrote this:

> Nealy has been a boy scout, an underground cartoonist (late 60's), high school dropout, war resister, civil rights activist, construction worker, college student (BA 1976), mountain rescue specialist, garbageman, professional rock musician (drummer), police analyst, sculptor, spelunker, motorcyclist, bowhunter, paramedic, canoeist, kayaker, river guide, fork-lift driver, parachutist, author (ten books translated into three languages), real estate photographer, yachtsman, sport angler, traditional archer, rollerblader, tree surgeon, environmental activist, and, occasionally, a drunk and drug addict. Plus a few other things we can't mention 'til the statute of limitations runs out. Also a political cartoonist, illustrator, private detective (2 arrests, 1 conviction, 1 pending), lifeguard, etc., etc. I've done more crazy-assed stuff than any other cartoonist on the fucking <u>planet</u>, period! And I still have enough brain cells to write books about my exploits.

Most of it, remarkably, more or less true.

At night after I was already in bed, I would hear them. William, Holly, their friends, all on the other side of the wall from me. They were trying to keep it down, but it was impossible for them. They were like ghosts to me: the disembodied laughter, the opening and closing of doors, the careful footsteps in the hallway, the lights from their departing cars sweeping through my window and across the ceiling. Then dark. Then silence. But it wasn't them who were the ghosts. I was the ghost, really, longing to be a part of their lives but unable to, and not because I was dead, but because my life had yet to begin. This is why I'm telling this story. This is when it starts.

The Missing Link

2 The Three of Us

May 21, 1972

ALTHOUGH I WAS thirteen years old, I think of this as the day I was born again, my coming-out party with Holly and William and . . . Alice Cooper. My first rock concert. Alice Cooper! Named for its singer who, it was said, would bite off the head of a chicken onstage and drink its blood. Who wore a live boa constrictor around his neck while decapitating baby dolls, and who, for an encore, would hang himself from a gallows. One of the early heavy metal bands, Alice Cooper learned early on that stagecraft was as important as the music they played. Their big hits, "I'm Eighteen," "Under My Wheels," and "School's Out," were loud, angry songs, sung in blistering screams by Vince Furnier, a.k.a. Alice. Blue Oyster Cult would be the opening act.

The concert was on the same night as Holly's senior prom (not William's: he had left high school without graduating). But the prom was a concept both of them found ridiculous. They went to it anyway, long enough to make an impression, leaving in time to pick me up and get to the show. William dressed as a gentleman serial killer, in a tux and top hat, his face framed by twin waterfalls of his long blond hair. Holly was a wraith, or maybe a corpse, her face painted white, with deep circles beneath her eyes. They could have been onstage.

I went as the little brother. The three of us watched Alice Cooper with his dripping mascara and baked-on sneer wrap the boa constrictor around his neck and hang himself onstage and scream as if he were the angriest man on Earth and hated us all. I wasn't really with William and Holly, though, not as much as I wanted to be; they were in the row behind me, smoking. The Birmingham Municipal Auditorium, already an old room when I was young, was so dark, with cracked concrete floors and sagging, weary gray chairs. I don't think they wanted to be seen with me: I was just a kid, after all. Through the first few minutes of Blue Oyster Cult, I was alone. But eventually Holly climbed over the seats and sat with me, and then William followed, one on either side, and I forgave them everything. They made me feel untouchable—so cool, a cool beyond what most people could even imagine.

For decades they were the absolute coolest, and as long as I was with them I thought I was, too. But you can't borrow *cool*. I was, at best, a sidekick. But over the course of the next few months, I sponged up all that I could. I started to wear torn T-shirts and frayed jeans. I let my hair grow to my shoulders, falling like a curtain over my eyes. I wore purple Converse tennis shoes and affected a mild disdain for just about everything. I didn't want to be Alice Cooper—he was too obvious, and obnoxious. All Alice Cooper wanted was your attention. I wanted to be William: quiet, removed, brave, fearless, skilled at everything, a man who could turn his experience not into a screed but into a cartoon. I wasn't William, though, and I never could be; I knew that, even then. And so, I did what I could with what I had. I picked the parts of him that suited me, the ones I could successfully acquire. I wanted to at least *seem* like him. I would never be the guy jumping off the roof, in other words, but I could do a good job acting like the guy who did.

How to dress a squirrel:

Cuffs 1½" to 2"— Cufflinks optional

Stripes or tiny patterns

Belt matches shoes

Pronounced break 2" to 3" above cuff

Charcoal or Navy pin-stripe.. Never brown!

3 The Secret Room

1972–1974

MY FATHER WAS a self-made man. He came from the small town of Cullman, Alabama, but left to make his fortune in what he called the "big pond" of Birmingham. He didn't have a college degree or any obvious skills, other than a winning smile, a head for numbers, and limitless ambition. He and my mother married in 1950. He was twenty years old, and she was eighteen. In 1951 my sister Rangeley was born, and then over the next nine years my mother and father had three more children: Holly, me, and my little sister Barrie.

My father's first forays into the business world were disastrous: he tried selling candles, roadside billboards, and cardboard reproductions of artistic masterpieces. I remember that Rembrandt's *Man with the Golden Helmet* was one of them. He failed time and time again but never stopped trying. Finally, in the sixties, he got a job selling Plaid Stamps, a rewards program. Customers received stamps at the checkout counter of supermarkets and other retailers and could later redeem them for products in a catalog. His experience there led him to create his own business, importing flatware and dishes from Japan, which were sold in supermarkets as well. In the same way Plaid Stamps encouraged you to shop at one retailer as opposed to another in order to get the stamps, his business—known as a continuity program—encouraged customers to shop at one particular grocery store chain to collect entire sets of flatware, cookware, china, and stoneware. After over a decade of trying and failing, finally he was successful, he had found his métier, and was at long last rich—or, as children of successful parents like to say, *we* were rich.

I was eleven when we moved from the small house on Mayfair Drive in Homewood to the much bigger one in the glitzy suburb of Mountain Brook. The new house had three floors and, of course, a pool. A year wouldn't pass before William would jump off that house into the pool and live to tell the tale, though he never told it. Jumping off roofs was something you did but didn't talk about having done, because that wasn't why you did it.

In the front yard monkey grass lined the flagstone walk to the porch. Two black concrete lions, each one the size of a three-year-old child, stood on either side of the door, perpetually roaring. Ivy climbed the white brick walls. Every yard in our neighborhood had a magnolia, pergolas draped with wisteria. On the hill across the street the houses were even bigger, palatial manors with long, winding driveways and lives of such fantastic elegance and wealth I could not even imagine. But our new house was sufficiently capacious, enough for me to have two rooms: one upstairs, where I had a double bed and a chest of drawers and a desk, where I could study and live like I was a kid, like any kid who had nothing to hide.

My other room was in the basement. It was out of the way, and not nearly as finished as the rest of the house was. No one had any use for it. The elderly couple who had lived here before us had used this room for their live-in help. The floor was concrete, and the walls were bare. In the adjoining bathroom, the toilet seat was made of wood and split in two places, and there was a claw-foot bathtub with a light brown waterline ring. It was bigger than any bathtub I had ever seen. There were two doors into the room. One was just a regular door to the hallway, but the other was a Dutch door. The top half could open while the bottom half stayed closed. This door led outside, and it was the door I would use when I wanted to go somewhere without telling anyone—when I wanted to sneak out.

This is the room where all the things that happened to me happened. It's where I had sex for the first time and where I taught myself to smoke cigarettes, both of which took long hours of sometimes arduous practice. It's where

I wrote my first song on guitar with my friend Jill, titled "Charades." *You can play charades if you want to / You can pull the shades and pretend you're not there.* It's where my high school friends and I would gather every Friday and Saturday evening to plan our forays into the night or decide not to go anywhere at all, just stay there, drink beer, smoke pot, listen to the *National Lampoon Radio Hour* and Van Morrison's third album, *Moondance. Moondance* seemed to be playing nonstop. In the hallway just outside the door, the room had its own small kitchen, with a stove and a refrigerator, and just a few feet away from that was the door to the pool.

It wasn't that the room itself was secret, of course, but much of what went on there was. Never once did my mother or father come down to see what I was up to, not when I was alone or when I was with my friends. They would open the door from the top of the stairs and call down to me for something, but I never saw their faces. They either trusted me or, because I was the third child, didn't want to bother as much anymore with hands-on parenting. I was probably going to be up to no good no matter where I was, and if that was the case, they would rather I be my worst at home. It was safer that way. But I really don't think they wanted to know.

I painted the walls in a wavelike pattern, yellow and blue. I tacked up pictures of rock stars. I took throw pillows from the couch upstairs and scattered them around the floor and smuggled in folding metal beach chairs from the garage. I didn't have any big plans for the room in the beginning; it was more like a tree house to me, although air-conditioned and without the tree.

But within a few months I had come up with a vision for it. I asked my mother for a waterbed. They were selling them down at the local head store, the Angry Revolt. I asked my mother because she could always be counted on to say yes, if only because she knew my father would have said no.

"That sounds like fun," she said. "Of course!"

She drove me down to the Angry Revolt, bought the bed and we brought it home, where I filled it with the hose just outside the Dutch doors. That night I tried to sleep on it, but I found that was impossible. The bed never stopped moving. It sloshed with every breath. It was exactly what sleeping on a bag full of water would feel like. I should have tried one out first before getting my mother to buy it, but that's not how I roll. To this day the idea of doing research about anything besets me; avoiding it is the source of most of the mistakes I've ever made.

Earlier that year William had borrowed my mother's white Camaro, opened the driver's side door and out of nowhere a car slammed into it, knocking the door clean off. A month before that he had dropped out of high school. He worked construction now. He actually kept his cigarettes in a pack rolled up in the sleeve of a short-sleeved T-shirt in what even then I thought he did ironically; but as a high school dropout and a construction worker, maybe he had earned it either way. As compelling as William, and his image, was to me, my father was repelled, in obvious and predictable ways. I can't imagine many fathers of a young, beautiful daughter would feel differently about William, though: he did look like trouble. I think no human creature could have been created who my father would have liked less. Holly had begun to spend time with him away from our house, but she never gave up trying to convince my father that William was worth a lot more than he appeared to be, often volunteering him for tasks around the house no one else could do, to try and prove it: leaky faucets and running toilets, installing door locks, mounting a new mailbox, rigging up a stereo unit in the family room.

So other than the coming and the going—mere glimpses after the day on the rooftop—I rarely saw William anymore. But then one day he just . . . showed up. There he was, outside of the door of my secret room. It was like a surprise appearance by a famous personality. For a moment I couldn't speak.

"Hey, dude," he said. Sunglasses, T-shirt, jeans, Converse. He wasn't smiling but he held his hand out for a low five. I gave it as if I'd given a million low-fives in my short life.

"Hey, William."

"Hear you're having some waterbed issues."

I nodded, grimaced. "It's like—"

"—a ride at the fair."

I nodded. He laughed as if he were quite familiar with this particular waterbed issue.

"Oh yeah," he said. "Mind if I take a look?"

"Sure," my voice not trembling with a giddy excitement, I'm sure. "Please. Yeah."

He walked into my room and took a look around. "You've really . . . made this your own," he said. He glanced at the posters. "Janis and Jimi. And who is that?"

"Duane Allman," I said. He was new to my wall.

"You just have pictures of dead people in your room? Kind of dark, dude," he said and laughed. "Hope they're not your role models."

"No," I said to my role model. "I just . . . like their music."

"Cool," he said, which was exactly the response I was going for. "Let's look at what we have here."

He studied the situation and it already seemed ridiculous to me: a bed made of water. Why would anyone want a bed made of water? And yet I had one.

"Well, you don't have enough water in there, first of all. You need about ten more gallons. And you need a frame."

"I didn't think about a frame."

"You're not the first person who didn't think about a frame," he said, "and you won't be the last."

I was thirteen years old; he was twenty. Hair parted in the middle, still down his shoulders. He was wearing sunglasses in the basement.

"Let's build a frame for this sucker," he said.

"Really?"

"I could not be more serious."

"Okay. Let's do it." My mind hit a wall. "How?"

"Nothing to it. I'll measure, get the wood cut, bring it back here and we'll knock it all together."

He had a tape measure hanging off the side of his belt, where a six-shooter might have hung had he been a cowboy. But even a tape measure exuded an exotic essence to me. He held out the silver end of the tape.

"Take this," he said, "and walk it to the other side of the bed."

He held on to the casing. I walked the end of the tape to the other side of the bed and stopped. He looked at the tape and wrote down a number on his hand with a pen. We did the same again in the other direction. He wrote that number down.

"Alright," he said. "I think we're all set. You can let go of the tape."

I let go of the tape and it was sucked back up into its casing and back on his belt in one quick, smooth motion. It was like a magic trick.

The next day he was back with four blond pieces of wood, two short, two long, and instead of the tape measure he had a hammer hanging from his belt, and in his other hand was a drill. In his pockets he packed screws and eight pieces of metal bent at an angle, each shaped like a little L.

"What are those?"

"L brackets," he said. "They'll hold it all together. We're not going to get too fancy."

But it was fancy to me. Putting things together, like jumping off a roof, was nothing I had ever seen a person do. I wasn't being raised to do that; I was being raised to make enough money to hire other people to do that. It's hardly a rare skill, I suppose, knocking a couple of pieces of wood together, but at the time it made a powerful impression. One of William's lists of things to do, which I would see much later, would daze me: *Decided not to kerosene tractor crankcase. Need to pull mower deck and get tractor about 12" in air to fix belt tensioner, drain axle and transmission.* What could that possibly mean? Once when I was ten I'd gone to a friend's house, and he walked me through his family's garage. Arranged across every wall were dozens and dozens of tools, from wrenches to mallets to chainsaws, all kinds of hammers, and implements the uses of which I had no idea. Torture, possibly.

"What is all this?" I'd said.

My friend gave me a look. He must have heard the wonder, and the fright, in my voice. "It's my dad's *work*shop," he said.

Now here was William, someone who could make things that hadn't existed in the world before he made them. That's what I admired, and would continue to admire, for the rest of his life. Had this facility for invention ended with the simplest of frames for my waterbed, I probably would have forgotten that incident by now. But ten years later, he cleared five acres of land and built a two-thousand-square-foot passive solar house on it, and then, inside it, drew maps of almost every major river in the Southeast. And of greatest importance was his art: out of nothing, he made ten books.

William could not have been more different from my father, but in one essential way they were the same: William was a self-made man, too.

But that time was far away and impossible to imagine then. He was just the disreputable boyfriend without a high school diploma trying to earn respect and affection by helping out the little brother; now there was just a drill, screws and L-brackets, a few pieces of wood. He gave me the screws and the L-brackets to hold and to hand to him when he was ready, and I found myself up to the challenge.

I took a step back as he started drilling, not that he would have noticed. He was focused, absorbed in the task before him. It was as if I had disappeared. That was fine: I didn't want to be directly involved in the actual construction of the frame, only in the social activity that surrounded it. I didn't want to learn; providing the screws and the L brackets was enough. He knew this, I think, even then, that I was not going to be much of a helper or a learner, but more of a watcher, and a dispenser of various paraphernalia. I don't think we talked at all that day outside of his requesting a screw or L bracket. Thirty years later and just six months before he died, William wrote that "Daniel drives me nuts . . . never volunteer help, can't/won't fix stuff, etc., etc., but he's golden . . ."

This was true. This is true.

I got him a beer from the fridge upstairs. In an hour, the job was done. My waterbed had a frame.

"Wow. Thank you," I said.

"It was nothing," he said. "My pleasure. A waterbed without a frame is very sad, dude."

I derived so much pleasure from hearing him use that word with me. *Dude.* Even though I always thought he used the word to be funny, or to make fun of people who used it without trying to be funny, it was a word friends used with friends. I knew I wasn't his friend. Not really, not yet. But it was a word I was hoping to grow into.

A couple of months after the frame was built, the waterbed sprang a leak, ruined my album collection and my rug, and I had to throw the bed away and I wasn't sad about it in the least. I hated that bed.

Now what? I needed something new in my life to absorb and distract me. I did not appear interested in being a self-made man, but rather was interested in having things made and done for me. William and my father both resented and disdained this quality in me. "Champagne taste, beer pocketbook," my father said of me, just like William's description of me, later, as a "golden" boy. I suppose they were both right. William and my father actually had so much in common: raised poor with alcoholic fathers, both were self-employed and self-starters. They had more in common with each other, I think, than either of them did with me.

Me, I just needed something to do, a distraction, or, as William would put it, "a new abyss to stare into."

I decided I needed a snake.

I don't know why I needed a snake; I felt no particular affiliation with them. It must have been for the simplest of reasons: I wanted one because I did not have one, no one I knew had one, and who, really, would ever want a snake, when there are so many other animals one could have? It was desirable in its undesirability. There was also the matter of Alice Cooper: *he* had a snake. He probably had several. They were beautiful and mysterious, I thought, as I peered at them through the panes of the pet store glass behind which they slithered and coiled, their coal-black beady eyes full of all the soulless evil in the world. I was drawn to the boa constrictor, sleek as a new car. It was the best snake, I thought, with the best snake name. *Boa constrictor* sounded exotic and dangerous. And it *could* constrict you, but at three-plus feet (the length of the one I had admired), it couldn't constrict you enough to do any real harm. It was like a too-firm handshake or being hugged around the neck by your overexcited four-year-old niece. Beautiful, too. Brown, creamy in places, with rusty-colored splotches up and down their long, perfect, simple bodies, devilishly bedazzled with subtly shiny scales.

Every night around seven my mother relaxed with a scotch on the rocks and a Salem. My father was usually out of town. That night, I said something complimentary about her hair or her shoes or just how generally wonderful she was.

"How sweet," she said.

"Mom," I said. "I was thinking about getting a pet."

"Really? That sounds like fun. A cat? A dog? You'd have to take care of it, you know."

"A boa constrictor."

"A what?"

"A snake."

"I know what a boa constrictor is."

"I was at the pet store—"

"Oh my God," she said. "Are you out of your mind? Seriously? That's the most outrageous thing I've ever heard come out of your mouth. But you're that age now, God help us."

"So, no?"

"No. No. A very big no, Danny, with bells on it."

Smoke plumed from her nostrils, like a dragon. She couldn't even look at me, her son who had wanted to bring a snake into the house.

"Jesus," she said.

William and Holly took me to the pet store the next day. William loved reptiles. Growing up, his mother said he could have anything as a pet "except a cat and a rhinoceros," and he took her up on it. "We had chameleons crawling on the living room drapery, snakes dozing in the bathtub of our only bathroom." Later in his life he would have two pet copperheads, which he would name Eddie 1 and Eddie 2, after his best friend Edgar was murdered. At the pet store, we window-shopped. There were several snakes to choose from, each coiled in its own aquarium near the back of the store. "Well?" he said. I pointed at one I liked. It was brown, gray, and cream, as thick as my wrist and as long as my arm. William checked it out like a used car. He held it. He let it curl around his shoulders, then his neck. He passed it over to me. I'd never felt anything like that: pure muscle. "That's a healthy snake," he said. "Maybe a little lethargic but who wouldn't be, in this place."

It was a go. Holly helped me pay for it, and we smuggled it into my secret room through the Dutch door. I installed a padlock on the hallway door in case, for some unknown reason, my mother ever wanted to see if I had a snake in my room. I named it Schlachthof, or "slaughterhouse," in German. I knew the word because I was reading *Slaughterhouse-Five* at the time, and I wanted to broadcast my literary prowess.

Schlachthof lived in an aerated plastic box for two days while William built a terrarium in the basement of his mother's home, where he was still living. The terrarium was four feet high and two feet square. There was a glass panel on one side, and the other three were made of plywood. The lid was on hinges with a latch on one side to prevent escape. Inside the terrarium there was a three-inch base of dirt, with rocks of various sizes scattered throughout. A small branch from a sweet gum tree was attached to the floor somehow, a mysterious and magical detail of construction that was beyond my ken. No matter: since William knew how to do this, there was no reason for me to know, too. Why would two people need to know the same thing?

I don't know why he built the cage for me; I don't know why he did any of the things he did for me over the years, other than that he could do them and that Holly doubtlessly encouraged him to. It may have been more for the snake than it was for me.

The terrarium was some of his finest work, an elegant home for a snake, but Schlachthof didn't seem to appreciate it. When I came home from school he would be asleep in a corner, coiled like a snake right out of central casting, and when he saw me, he would raise his head wearily, and then, unimpressed, lower it. Once out of the cage he was more active, twining himself around my arm or my neck. I never felt my life was in danger; he was easy to disentangle if his hold felt too tight. But the idea that people thought he could possibly hurt me enhanced that distinctive quality of weirdness that I was trying so hard to cultivate. I was the guy who had the snake. We hung out together in my secret room. He was my pal. He only bit me a couple of times. When friends would come by to see him, I acted as though Schlachthof was only *truly* comfortable with me, so please be careful holding him, et cetera, because he was, after all, a boa constrictor! I had asked William about it, if he thought Schlachthof really did know me and recognize me as his human. He thought it over.

"Probably not by sight, but by smell. The way most people recognize you."

He sort of smiled. William had made a joke with me! I laughed. We were, like, making jokes. That was pretty awesome.

Schlachthof's diet consisted of mice, or was supposed to. When we bought him we had also purchased a small metal mouse cage with two mice in it.

"All he has to eat is one a week," William said that first day, as I watched the mice clutch at the bars of their cell, begging for freedom in the most endearing possible way. Mice do make expressions, somehow, with their little black eyes. They looked pitiful, desperate, pleading. "Just drop one in there and watch nature take its course."

I carefully unlatched the top of the cage and captured the one that had foolishly cowered in a corner. I lifted him by his hairless tail.

I paused. "I just . . . drop him in?"

"Just let the little sucker go, and the circle of life will begin."

I did. He landed in the dirt on all fours and quickly took in his new digs. He didn't move, paralyzed by the three-foot-long boa a mere foot away. Easy prey. Schlachthof played it cool, though, pretending not to see him; this is what snakes did. I imagined this moment of serpentine nonchalance would lead to the sudden, faster-than-lightning strike. William and I watched. One minute became two, three; the mouse, true to form, turned and ran. But Schlachthof made not a move toward him.

"What's wrong?"

William shrugged. He assumed a studious look. He took a deep breath, working through the possibilities. "He probably had dinner before we picked him up, and so he might not be hungry for a few days. Just leave the mouse in there. At the very least, it'll be company for him while you're at school."

Days passed, then a week, and the mouse made himself at home. He wandered around the terrarium aimlessly, sometimes inches from the tip of Schlachthof's nose. I took some pellets from the cage where the other two mice seemed, in comparison, happy, and dropped it in to him, feeding food to my snake's food, in the very arena of its impending death.

But the mouse didn't die, at least not then. After a week, the mouse realized it had nothing to fear from Schlachthof, and he had his run of the place. He walked past Schlachthof's deadly jaws without a second look. Maybe Schlachthof was depressed. I got him out as often as I could. I let him nap with me under the covers. But nothing worked. I didn't know how to raise the spirits of a depressed snake.

Then one day I came home and discovered that the mouse, far from being eaten, had actually bitten Schlachthof on the nose. My snake had two small red marks right by his nostrils. This was terrible and literally unbelievable. What kind of snake *was* he?

I had to protect my boa constrictor. I removed the mouse and returned it to the little cage.

William stopped by and I told him what had happened.

"Oh, wow," he said. "The mouse actually bit your snake. That's insane."

"I know. What do I do?"

This is what William was for, for me and for everybody else, then and for the rest of his life. He was there to solve mysteries, settle disputes, build things, fix them when they broke. *What do I do? How do I do it? How long does it take? What is it called?* He had all the answers. He was like an iPhone: there was no reason to learn anything or do anything yourself when it was so easy to get solutions from someone who had already gone to the trouble.

He shook his head. I could tell it wasn't good news. "Dude," he said. "Here's the thing. The snake needs protein to live, same as we all do. But if it's not going to eat, you're going to have to feed it."

He told me I would need to get a syringe, and some egg yolk. Then he showed me how to open the snake's jaw with my thumb and forefinger and how to squirt a syringe full of slimy orange yolk down its throat.

"Once or twice a week should do it," he said, "and Schlachthof will probably outlive us all."

"Great," I said, with zero enthusiasm.

It wasn't long after this that I asked William if he'd like to have Schlachthof. By this time, he and Holly had moved into a tiny apartment in Southside, a little bit bigger than a walk-in closet. Southside was cheap, dangerous, the opposite of my home in Mountain Brook where nothing bad was ever supposed to happen to anybody.

But sure, he said, of course: there is always room for a snake. I think he'd expected this to happen, actually, that eventually I'd just give up and he'd step in. He took the snake away, and the truth is I didn't miss him very much: my passions were powerful but fleeting.

William must have felt like such a stranger in our family. He was from the tribe of people who repurposed and fixed things; we were from the tribe who forsook things, who threw them away when they ceased fulfilling their advertised or desired purpose. It's easier, abandoning what doesn't work the way you want it to, whether it's a bed or a snake or a person; the world is lighter when you let things go and move on. But William didn't let things go, no matter what they were. His background was in the Boy Scouts, and I think he took the oath of the Scouts and internalized it: "to help other people at all times." He always tried to make things work. He took on the ballast. This is the gift my family gave him: all that extra weight. Even Holly, the woman he loved, would end up weighing him down. He became earthbound, mortal, and I think that was because of our family.

Even after William left for college, his persona informed so much of who I became in high school, and who I thought I wanted to become. My best friend (whom I'll call Marvin in the interest of protecting his early history) and I would spend long afternoons dividing small bales of marijuana into one-ounce baggies, for sale and distribution at the private school we attended. I didn't sell it, that was Marvin's job; I just provided the secret room where the merchandise could be cleaned and bagged. It was 1974. This job—pot dealer—had been handed down to Marvin by his cousin, who had in turn received it from his cousin; it was a family business. Marvin and I broke up the pounds and, in the tradition of the time, separated out the seeds and stems with the inside covers of our double albums, where the seeds rolled to the crease. After they were weighed and packaged, he took them home, leaving a garbage bag full of stems and seeds beneath my post-waterbed bed—a traditional single mattress with box springs and a frame.

William found me here when he came back to Birmingham. He'd been gone for a year and a half, auditing classes at Oxford in England and then to college at St. John's in New Mexico, who'd accepted him even though he didn't have a high school diploma. Of course, he joined their search and rescue team. "We learned how to rappel, treat hypothermia, splint broken bones and, in general, how to deal with wilderness trauma (usually our own!)." It was also where he would read the classics. He'd come back when his father died and now lived back in Southside, with Holly.

He was a drummer so he'd knock on the door the way a drummer might, with some distinctive *bop bop de bop*, and, opening the door, peer through with an expression of innocent expectancy.

"What's going on, dude?"

Me: shrugging. Gesturing toward a book or the blue-lined notebook where I'd taken notes from classes that day. "Not much."

"Permission to enter?"

"Sure, yeah, great."

Part of growing up is pretending not to care about things you care about quite a lot. I pretended not to care whether he was here. Shrugging, lazy-eyed, laid-back, I'd wave him in like a mob boss to his flunky. He'd be dressed in a variation of the same clothes he wore almost every day for his entire life: a T-shirt and jeans, tennis shoes or boots, hair pulled back in a ponytail. Stuffed into one of his back pockets: a paperback. Where the waterbed had once leaked, there was now a beanbag chair and a corner piled high with throw pillows. Now I had photos of Fats Domino and Waylon Jennings and Eric Clapton on my wall.

He'd get on the bed and lean into a pillow.

I knew why he was here but both of us tried to allow for a polite conversational buffer before we got to it.

"How's school?"

Shrug. "It's okay, I guess."

"You still playing basketball?"

"Yeah." Though I loved playing basketball, I feigned disinterest. Was there anything less cool than playing high school basketball at a private school? "We have a game on Tuesday. Against Briarwood Christian."

"I should come and see you play. Holly said you're amazing."

Holly had actually never seen me play basketball, though, and imagining William and Holly in our tiny gym, on the bleachers beside the wax-figure parents come to cheer for their children, was a scene almost impossible to imagine.

"That would be cool."

I struggled to say something more, but the fear of revisiting later what I said now and being mortified by it was overwhelming, and so I said next to nothing. William didn't share very much information about his life either and I didn't ask for any, and maybe this is where the ground rules for the rest of our lives were set: Don't ask questions. Talk as sparingly as possible. Do something, do *anything*, instead. So we would play pool, ride bikes, drink, smoke, do drugs, play music occasionally, go to bars, fish. But not much in the way of talking.

"Do you still have that magic bag?" he said, finally getting to the reason for his visit, which I already knew.

"Sure do."

I leaned forward, reached under the bed and pulled it out. William slipped to the floor and leaned against the bed frame, and I sat cross-legged on the beanbag chair. I poured part of the bag onto the *White Album*, as the eponymous ninth studio album by the Beatles was commonly called.

"Birmingham is dry as a bone," he said.

I looked at the bare and prickly stems, a bramble bush of them, the seeds rolling off the album onto the floor. "We're down to the dregs here, too," I said.

"Better the dregs than nothing at all."

We combed through the garbage bag. Two weeks ago, it had been easy to get a joint or two off the leftover stems, and last week it was down to a bowl. Soon there would be nothing at all. We spent a good long time going through the bag together, because even when you thought you'd gone through it all, there was always something left, at least until there wasn't. William found enough for a hit, maybe two. He brushed it into a little pouch he kept in his front pocket.

"This okay?" he said.

"Yes, sure, of course."

"Well," he said, and sighed. "Thanks. It appears that the magic bag may be done for."

"Looks like it."

"Until the next shipment then."

"Yep."

He stood, unfolded himself, stretched, yawned.

"Alright, buddy. I will be in touch."

No hugs, no handshakes, no high fives. He was gone. And it was okay that it happened like that because that's what friends do: they check in, they see what's up, ask how you are and shoot the shit. But I didn't think he was there to shoot the shit with me, not really: he was there because I had something he wanted. If it hadn't been for the magic bag, he wouldn't have been there at all, I thought. Was there anything so wrong with that, though? Everyone wants something from somebody, even if it's just the last of the stems and seeds. Pot was a gateway drug to my friendship with William—these early days a dim precursor to the more serious pursuits to follow. Because nothing is merely trans- actional; something other than the thing itself is always exchanged.

But maybe there was something else. Because then he was back, *bop de bop bop*, leaning through the half-open door.

"I forgot," he said. "Made this for you."

He stepped in and handed it me. It was a hollowed-out Jenga tile with a pipe bowl dug deep into it on one end covered by part of a pop-top from a Coke can as a carburetor, a small hole drilled through the other end to pull from. It was the first and only homemade pipe I ever had.

I still have it. In the museum of my life, this pipe may be the sole remaining artifact from that era, the early days with William, the last vestige of my secret room.

4 The Man with No Name

Summer 1973

WILLIAM AND I went to the movies once, just the two of us. I was fourteen years old; William, twenty-one. It was the first time I had been with him out in the world without Holly. He took me to see a Clint Eastwood triple feature matinee at the Green Springs 4, the biggest theater in town, on Green Springs Highway, out on the edge of nowhere. I don't know why he took me.

He wore his gray leather jacket. The jacket looked like it had been through a war or two. It was loaded with zippers, four big pockets, two on each side. In each pocket he'd smuggled in a beer. There was no one else in the theater, for some reason—not a soul. Just us. A chance private screening. We watched the three Eastwood movies in a row: *A Fistful of Dollars, For a Few Dollars More,* and *The Good, the Bad and the Ugly.* We moved in close, fourth row from the front, and for the next six hours hardly spoke. Neither did Clint. He just rode around on his horse with that sad, hard countenance, shooting people who deserved to be shot, saving people who deserved to be saved, smoking a cigarillo. He isn't even given a name in these movies, and that's why his character is called "The Man with No Name." When William handed me one of his four beers, my first, he didn't say anything weird or uncool like *Don't tell your mother.* He just handed it to me and leaned back into the seat with his boots on the seat in front of him and watched the movie. I don't know how much of the movie I watched, much of my attention being absorbed by where I was and who I was doing it with, the appreciation of this new fact of my life, that I was in a theater, watching a triple feature, sitting next to William. Drinking a beer. The beer was bitter, almost undrinkable. Like cigarettes, it took a lot of time and practice to get past the baseline of its essential awfulness. But I relished it.

I watched the movies, but I also watched William. I watched him to see how he sat in his chair, how he slumped, where he put his feet, how he held a can of beer—how to *be,* in other words, how to be William—while he did the same thing with Clint. Like what I saw in him, William recognized in Eastwood a kinship he wanted to nurture. In those early movies, Eastwood's characters were strong, quiet, detached, basically good men who seemed to have been hurt somehow, badly hurt in a way they couldn't talk about with anybody, even with the women they loved. All they could do was live outside the stream of life, coming to the rescue of a damsel in distress now and again, to help a friend out of a jam, to get justice, revenge if necessary. Characters who didn't want to hurt anybody but would— and could—if provoked. Lonely and haunted, with the same enigmatic and taciturn detachment. But on the side of the angels, yes, at least most of the time.

I don't know what happened to "The Man with No Name" to turn him into the wounded thing he had become, and for a long time I didn't know what made William *William*, either. He was like—would become like—so many things, so many different heroes and antiheroes to me. A proto-geek on a motorcycle, Holly's arms around his waist holding on for dear life, or swinging a pair of nunchucks, smoking a cigarette.

He had a code. I don't know that I would call it a "moral" code, but something like that. Maybe it was drawn from Hemingway, following the ideals of courage and endurance and measuring himself against the challenging situations he endured. Maybe that was why he became a paramedic and an EMT by the time he was twenty-one; maybe that was why he slept with a police scanner on his bedside table, hoping to hear of a tragedy he was singularly qualified to help with. Or why he would risk his life as a *way* of life, and why, despite the sometimes-dark detachment (especially toward the end), despite the guns in the secret cutaway wall in the bathroom that I would learn about later, despite the para-military esprit of his imaginary life—despite all that—he never, ever hurt a living soul, never could and never did. Just himself. I thought of him as the child of James Dean, Albert Camus, Ernest Hemingway, Keith Richards, Satan, G.I. Joe, and of course, Clint Eastwood. That was the part he played, anyway, that was the disguise he wore—courageous, sure, but not competitive, not aggressive. He was self-conscious about it, too, and often made fun of the macho masquerade, especially in his drawings.

"I thought of William as a trick mirror," a friend of his, Virginia, said later. "There was this visage that he showed to the world, and then there was this vast rabbit hole that opened up into the interior of William that we could not see, because we were just getting this veneer."

At the end of the triple-feature he drove us back to my house, sharing not a word. There was so much to talk about, too: life and death and how to suffer through both with strength and dignity. Is it ever right to take the life of another human being? What was going on behind Eastwood's eyes? We could have talked about that, but we didn't, and now I see this excursion as the beginning of my training. I was learning that simply because you had feelings and ideas it did not mean you had to share them, especially when you were with someone else who was having ideas and feelings of their own. The complicit silence. Sharing pieces of who you are is a muscle that requires training, and early on I learned from William to dispense with that. If Clint Eastwood could go five hours without talking, surely we could go fifteen minutes.

He let me out at the top of the driveway.

"Later, dude."

And he drove away, car lights swallowed up by the dark.

At one of his memorial services twenty-eight years later I would say this:

> Before he finally became my brother-in-law, William
> was my outlaw brother. He was dangerous and
> beautiful and he showed me around. He was the
> ringmaster of my world. Smart and strong without
> fear. Still, he could care for what was most elegant
> and fragile. Some of the things he taught me about
> were art, love, and how to catch, clean, and gut
> a fish. Ever since I can remember, if ever I had a
> decision to make about almost anything in the world,
> I pretended to be him for a minute. And I would ask
> myself, "What would William do?"
>
> I could get a T-shirt made with these words
> on it, and bumper stickers. And then start a little

mail-order business and eventually I'd have a
following. A cult, with William at the center of it. I
don't know if I could actually do this, but he could. I
love him, and I miss him, and I always will.

I meant it, at the time.

Swimming Self-rescue, cont'd..

It's easy to get disoriented while being trashed in a good-sized hole. Open your eyes... look around....
Lots of bubbles mean "HOLE"!
Look for the darker less-aeriated water that signifies the down-stream flow.

Above all,

Don't

Give

Up!

Once in non-aeriated water swim towards the light.

You might get lucky...

5 His Origin Story

Fall 1965

I HEARD THIS story from an old friend of William and Holly's, Nabb Quinn. William had visited Nabb in Atlanta when Nabb was about to get married. He and his fiancée were living together, and they had a pool, and William took advantage of it. He was born to be in the water. Nabb's fiancée watched William swim, and when he got out, in his cutoffs, dripping, she kept watching him as he walked toward the house, grabbed a towel, dried off. He walked past her and went inside. Later that night in bed, she told Nabb that she had never seen a better-looking man than William. Never.

"My fiancée told me that," Nabb said, laughing. "My fiancée. Because, you know, it was true."

Nabb also told me the story of the night William met Death for the first time, a story he heard from another Scout who was there, Richard B.

There were two deaths, actually: the Fogelman twins, who died just a few feet away from William. He was the last to see them alive, the first to see them dead.

William was a member of Scout Troop 57. Every month the troop went on camping trips, and once a year they went to the Big Ditch. The Big Ditch was in Gordo, Alabama, about halfway between Tuscaloosa and Columbus, Mississippi. By all accounts, the Big Ditch was just that—a big hole in the ground, something like a sinkhole, thirty feet deep. The soil was a mixture of sand and clay. Running through the middle of the hole was a ridge about three feet wide that spanned the length of it, and on either side of the ridge was a precipitous and direct drop into the canyon. The Scouts camped about twenty-five yards away, and that's where they would sleep, too, but as long as there was light they played in the Big Ditch, having dirt fights and chasing each other around, rolling down the steep inclines into the soft mud below. Sometimes pieces of the ditch would erode and fall away, like an iceberg, calving.

A feature of the ridge at the top of the Big Ditch: one end sloped upwards for about ten feet, and at the top of the slope was a ledge. To get there you had to dig footholds. It wasn't an easy climb, especially in the soft and crumbly soil. Troop 57 was going to play Capture the Flag later in the day, and some of the Scouts determined that an ideal place to hide the flag would be at the top of the slope, on the ledge, in the back of a pocket they dug into the clay and sand embankment.

But it was more than just a pocket. They dug and dug until they made a tunnel, almost a little cave. They created a roof under which the Scouts were sheltered. As the game and the digging progressed, from afternoon and into the evening, four Scouts were left digging beneath the overhang:

the brothers Jerry and Jimmy Fogelman, William's best friend Richard B., and William.

The Scouts had flares they would set off occasionally for light to work by when the dark came on, but pretty soon they ran out of flares and so, other than the stars above, there was no light at all. William knew every constellation by heart, of course. He could name them all.

By nine it was country-dark, no lights from any city to cast even a milky glow into the blackness. The Scouts still careened up and down the soggy ditch. They must have looked like little baby mud-monsters. The game was in progress. They were after the flag, but it was so well protected. It took some time.

And then it just happened, the overhang collapsed. A boulder hidden inside it fell directly on the Fogelman twins, crushing and suffocating them. Richard, the best friend, was buried in the heavy dirt and clay, too. It didn't take long for it all to begin, and then for it to end—a brief and sudden shock of cracking, crumbling earth—but it took a few moments for the other Scouts—still playing in the pit— to realize what had happened. And it was so dark. But once they realized what had happened, they started climbing the side of the ridge. Frantically. Crawling up, falling back.

Richard was the first to be seen and rescued. He had placed one hand over his mouth, forming an air pocket. The other hand, uncovered, he was waving above the dirt. A

Scout who was there dug Richard out. "That's when I heard another boy screaming," he said. "'Everybody is dead! Everybody is dead!'"

That boy was William.

It was unclear whether William had been buried in the collapse of the cave he helped create, or partially buried, or was somehow spared. It was so dark. None of the Scouts I spoke to knew what had actually happened to him. Just that he was screaming, and that somehow he knew that the Fogelman twins were dead, and there was nothing he could do for any of them.

The twins were in open caskets at their funeral, buried in their Scout uniforms. "I remember having to view them in the caskets with my dad," the former Scout said. "I really didn't want to as it hurt me so much thinking of the horror that night and the nightmares. I always dreamed of falling off that ledge and not being able to climb back up because the sand and rocks kept pushing me off those little handholds. Always hearing the screams of whoever it was screaming up there."

The Scout kept the Fogelmans' obituary taped to his dresser mirror for weeks, until his mother took it down. "You don't need to think about that anymore," she said.

William himself never once mentioned this night to me. I first heard about it in 2017, secondhand from Nabb. Richard B. told Nabb how he was sure he was going to die. How he remembers seeing the four of them floating above their bodies. The Fogelman twins, Richard, and William. "It was the greatest sense of peace and well-being I have ever felt in my life," Richard said.

Richard B. is still alive, but he's off the grid. He has no email address, no computer; bills come in his mother's name. As far as the world goes, he doesn't exist. Richard B. and William had been friends since childhood—his partner in pranks. Nabb tried to get Richard to talk with me, but he wasn't interested. "My relationship with William," Richard said, "is between me and William, and not fodder for the entertainment of others."

I don't know. My theory was that this night shaped William as if he were made of the same loamy clay as the Big Ditch itself. It struck me as the through line connecting the Before and the After of his life. He was spared but had to watch as Richard and the twins disappeared beneath the crumbling ceiling of the earth. He saw the boulder crush the twins, and before Richard was able to get his hand out of the dirt to wave, William had started screaming—*Everyone is dead!*—and couldn't stop, even when he saw that Richard was alive. There was nothing William could do but scream.

But all that would change. This would be the last time he would stand by helplessly and watch as his friends died. It was why he would become an amateur geologist: to understand where in the world it was safe enough to stand. It was why he became a medic and a mountain climber. It was why he tried to save my sister's life for decades, and why he would spend a year of his own trying to bring the man who he thought killed his best friend to justice. He was a hero, and he was a hero because he did heroic things, while beneath it all there was just that boy, dressed in a Scout's uniform covered in mud, screaming.

This book is dedicated to my "special friend", Holland Wallace

Without whom life itself would be impossible....

---

6 A Kind of Love Story

I COULD COMPARE them to Romeo and Juliet (love, death, tragedy). Or maybe they were more like Odysseus and Penelope: William off on his death-defying adventures, Holly surrounded by suitors, awaiting his return. Burton and Taylor: a fierce attachment marked by brutal betrayals and occasional reprisals. Bonnie and Clyde: partners in crime. They were my entry into this pantheon of dramatic lovers, their decades-long attachment proving that love, like water, can keep you alive for a very long time, although not forever. But specifically, this kind of love. It's another thing I wanted that was his, that was theirs.

In the summer of 1964, they were just kids who happened to live in the same neighborhood. One day Holly—dark brown hair, bangs, cheeks spotted with freckles—wandered into William's backyard, where he was playing with matches and gasoline. Literally playing with matches and gasoline.

Imagine him looking up, seeing Holly heading straight for him. Lightning fast, she snatched the matches away and she stuck them in her little girl's purse.

"You could kill yourself," she said—she really said this, the most prophetically ironic statement ever made by an eleven-year-old in history.

According to Holly, her purse somehow burst into flames. She also said that later that summer he stole her bicycle and sold it to someone for ten dollars, because boys just did that sort of thing sometimes.

This is how they came to know each other.

Years passed. In high school they ran with different crowds for a while. In high school Holly wore skirts so short they'd send her home to change; William dropped out. Holly was dating a drummer named Johnny and the story she told is that Johnny asked his friend William to hang out with her—keep an eye on her, you know—while he was playing.

William kept an eye on her. Did he ever.

William would later start playing the drums himself.

From then on it was never just William, never just Holly. It was always *WilliamandHolly*. One without the other never worked.

Not that they didn't try.

After he dropped out of high school—this would be in 1968 or 1969—William worked construction jobs, an artist with a hammer and a nail, while reading his doomsaying philosophers with the hard-to-spell names (Kierkegaard, Nietzsche), and, in spite of his asthma, smoking as if he were being paid by the cigarette. Just over a decade later he would use the skills he acquired to design and build that solar-powered home for Holly and him on twenty acres of land in the North Carolina countryside, by which time his asthma had progressed to the point that he would wake up sometimes unable to breathe, as if someone had stuck a wet sock down his throat. It was a beautiful home, with a gazebo and a pool and a hot tub, a country resort. Sometimes they called it Club Ned.

They weren't monogamous, not in high school or in college or for years after that. It's not that kind of love story. One summer William left her for a girl named Celeste. He and Celeste drove halfway across the country together before he realized the error of his ways and returned. Holly forgave him after going away with another man to Florida for a couple of weeks. They were even.

It wasn't until they settled into a life in the country and their age and ailments got the better of them that their outside interests diminished and finally ended. But even before then, when they split they always came back together, and seemed so strong, if not stronger, when they did. After one nearly final breakup, William took two nickels and placed them on a railroad track where they were flattened by a train. He drilled a hole into the nickels and they each wore one around their necks on a leather cord for the rest of their lives. They made mistakes and then made up for them. This only heightened my desire to create something like they had, an eternal bond with room for error.

They had so many stories. Like how one summer in 1969 when William was seventeen and Holly was sixteen, they were on a motorcycle he'd borrowed from a friend who'd stolen it from somebody else. The wind blew their hair out of the back of their helmets like streamers. They weren't going anywhere in particular and could feel the day spread out before them. He pulled over to a phone booth in front of a Quick Stop to call a friend.

There was a condominium complex next to the Quick Stop. The door to one of the condos was ajar. They slipped in to explore. It was furnished, immaculate, the bed big, so inviting. They had a quick tryst. Afterward, they found bathrobes in the closet and spent the next hour in the living room, as if they owned the place.

Then the realtor appeared with some clients.

The realtor was calm but looked like he wanted to shoot them. "These guys were going to sign the contract today," he said. He held them there until the deputies appeared and cuffed them.

"Holly is an intelligent, danger-loving sex bomb. Wow," William would write of her in his journal. "Irritating, demanding, powerful, but, wow."

They left Birmingham in '72 to attend different schools but found their way back to each other. They then both enrolled at Birmingham Southern College, shared an apartment off campus, eventually graduated. They took acid, smoked pot, etc. They rock climbed and hiked in the plateau country of northern Alabama. Then they bought a canoe from a good friend, Tom Schlinkert, who had just opened the Liquid Adventure canoe shop in town. "On our maiden voyage," William wrote, "we wrapped our new canoe around a tree on a floodstage river, nearly drowning in the process. This was extremely exciting . . . we were hooked!" It changed his life.

He seemed to live in our pool after that, learning how to roll a kayak. Rolling a kayak entails sitting in it, turning upside down underwater, and then using the paddle and a hip-snap to turn it right-side up. He'd be there for hours, learning this move and then others. Sometimes it worked, he'd flip right-side up, but often he would be upside down under water for what felt like a very long time.

Weeks passed between visits, and every time I saw them next, Holly and William were the same but also just a little different, older, not as present, less like older children and more like young adults. It's the natural order of things: people grow up and go away.

Then my sister Holly turned to stone and everything stopped.

A few months after she turned twenty-one, Holly woke up one morning unable to move. She had rheumatoid arthritis. It began with her hands and feet, and then spread to her knees, ankles, wrists, shoulders. Eventually it would spread to her lungs and heart, to the nerves themselves. Years later she would be on the cover of *Newsweek*, becoming the unlucky but beautiful face of the disease. But that wouldn't happen for decades; now, at twenty-one, this ossification was just the promise of what was to come. Through it all, though, she would persevere with a zany humor and an immersion into the medicine and the science behind her illness. She knew, at times, more than the doctors treating her did.

But the disease would overtake her eventually. This was clear to everybody. The week it happened, she moved back home and stayed in my room, upstairs.

It would have made so much sense for William to leave her. It's what my parents expected. All he wanted was to be outside, climbing on things, sloshing around in the water, riding a motorcycle, keeping an eye open for unlocked condo doors. A risk-taker is what he was. He wanted to get as close as he could to disaster, but then, through wit and skill, unflinchingly, get right out of it. It's what drew him to climbing mountains, running rivers, and eventually biking down muddy trails through the woods: there was danger there, but it was danger you could prepare for. You could die, doing these things, and people did, but you wouldn't, not if you were capable and careful and smart. You could live very close to that last unknowable moment, that edge, and get through it. This is where he was meant to be.

My father just thought William was a loser, but he was, at heart, just a boy. He spent the rest of his life writing and drawing about being a boy, trying to perfect it. He was an Eagle Scout with addiction problems, a genius who was happier in a tree than a classroom. Everything he did—from drawing cartoons, rafting rivers, riding bicycles, inline skating, climbing mountains and trees—trees, for God's sake!—are the pastimes of a kid. And he was lucky, because for a long time he had the perfect accomplice in my sister, an adventuress from a rich family, a mountain-climbing kayaker herself, game for anything from high-water rafting to heroin. She was *so game*. Even after she got arthritis and couldn't hold a paddle, they taped her hands to the stirrups in a canoe and let her shoulders do the work, which is why she had to get two shoulder replacement surgeries a few years down the line, *and then a replacement for one of the replacements*. In her fifty-eight years she would have five different shoulders. And if she had to do it all again, she said, she would.

He could have left her, and hearts would have been broken. But hearts are broken all the time. He didn't leave her, though, because despite everything he was and would become, he loved her. He was a caretaker and a problem-solver. He didn't toss something away because it was broken; he tried to fix it. He tried to save her. For the next twenty-five years he made almost every home-cooked meal they ever ate, and cleaned up after it, too. He took her places she would have never been able to go without him. He was a born adventurer who became a nurse to the woman he loved most in the world. Even knowing what he knew, what I now know, I think he would do it again.

7 Sally

IN 1976, THE outdoor store Liquid Adventure opened a small outpost on the Locust Fork River in northern Alabama. William helped build it, guided canoe trips, and drew his first cartoon T-shirts for the shop. Holly's arthritis was in remission, for the summer at least, and she was able to steer and paddle a canoe. Northern Alabama is the most conservative part of a very conservative state. There was an immediate and severe culture clash between the locals and what they called "the river hippies." The latter's cars were vandalized, barbed wire was strung across rapids, and finally the shop itself was burned down, KKK posters nailed to the ruins. Holly and William decided to leave Alabama altogether and take a trip across America in William's van to look for another place to live. They disappeared from my life for the whole year.

I did what I could to hold down the fort. I wasn't William, but I did what I could. I wasn't brave, artistic, or strong or even all that bright, but I was able to maintain a level of drug intake that he would have admired. By the time I was fourteen I had been taking LSD almost every weekend for a year, sometimes with friends and sometimes alone.

I remember Eric G., a friend from those years, marveling at me.

"I think you're breaking some records," he said, as if it were a competition.

He was right. Holly had told me stories of how she and William would wake up around 4 a.m., drop acid, go back to sleep, and wake up in a new world. I never did that. But one weekend when my parents went out of town and the house was empty, I dropped too late and was up all night long. I found a copy of *Even Cowgirls Get the Blues* on a shelf and read it cover to cover, finishing as the sun came up. My best friend Marvin and I took a tab on the first day of basketball practice with our new coach, Mr. Jolly. Every morning, Marvin's cousin drove us to school in his beat-up blue Chevy; he'd pull up in front of my house and honk. When I opened the passenger door a cloud of smoke would escape as if something inside were on fire. By the time we got to school we'd be baked. I had other friends I'd spend long afternoons with, fingers deep in cow patties, searching for psilocybin mushrooms. Looking back now it seems like a constant thing—the quest for drugs. I maintained other obsessions, though: there was basketball and banjo and listening to live music. I could fill pages with the names of the bands I saw by myself and with my friends. So stoned once, I wandered backstage at a Ten Years After concert, was thrown out of the show, and had to sit outside on the curb until my mother came to pick me up, two hours later. These are all the skills I had acquired, that and shoulder-length brown hair, a sullen disposition, and a small but stalwart group of friends.

Then I fell in love with a girl named Sally. Sally was sweet and funny, smart, blond, brown-eyed, and smoked Marlboro Reds she'd sometimes roll up in the sleeve of a T-shirt like a biker. She was just a wisp of a girl. She was an alcoholic, too, the first binge drinker I ever knew. She wore red calico shirts and blue jeans. She'd drive over to my house after school, in her antique white Volvo, and we'd hang out in the living room for a while, sometimes with my mother or my sister. Then we'd go upstairs and watch television or do homework or make out and, after a few months of this, sleep together.

My parents loved her. She was such a bright spirit and seemed to make me happy. She crocheted God's Eyes for all of us. It was fine with them if she spent the night, and once or twice a week she did. She'd tell her parents she was spending the night with her best friend, Brenda. Sometimes my father would bring us orange juice in the morning, waking us up just in time for school. That didn't seem odd at the time and only seems so now, as I'm writing it down. My sister Rangeley chalks it up to "the age of Aquarius and Women's Lib. Anything conventional was boring to them, stupid."

When she wasn't with me, Sally drank a lot. Not as much with me because I didn't drink that much, and even as a kid I was judgmental and had lofty standards I applied to everyone who was not me: taking drugs was age-appropriate;

drinking felt like something my parents did. Drunks seemed less interesting than stoners. With her other friends, Sally would drink until she passed out. She couldn't go home like that and so one of her friends, this pack of serious drinkers she spent her other life with, would bring her over to my house to sleep it off. This might be at ten or eleven at night, or later. She was light enough to carry, so I took her in my arms upstairs to my room, and in the morning she'd wake up not knowing how she'd gotten there, and cry. When she was a baby, she told me, her parents had given her a spoonful of whiskey at night to put her to sleep and then a spoonful of coffee in the morning to wake her up.

I told her that she drank too much and had to stop. But she couldn't, or wouldn't, and was afraid I'd break up with her because of it. And this was exactly what I did.

I did it the summer after we graduated, in 1977, before she went away to college to the University of Alabama, just an hour away from Birmingham. She pleaded with me not to break up with her because she loved me, but it was for the best, I told her. She was going away to college and needed to start her new life without a boyfriend in the background. I used every platitude I could find. You need to be free, I said.

But I don't *want* to be free! She said that over and over. *I don't want to be free.*

I set her free anyway. The truth is, of course, I was the one who wanted to be free. I was the one who didn't want a girlfriend in the background, a potential roadblock in my as-yet-unknown adventures. I'd been with her so long, almost two whole years: who knew what I was missing? As William wrote in a journal, "I'm such a romantic that I won't do one thing because then I'd miss out on X number of alternate experiences . . ." I was just that sort of romantic myself, the kind that sacrifices romance for nothing at all.

Later that fall Sally traveled back to Birmingham for a party. I was still in Birmingham because I'd decided to take a gap year and work for my father in his warehouse, driving a truck, living at home. She didn't tell me she was coming, and why would she? She was free. The car she was in veered off the road and onto the shoulder. The car tumbled and rolled. No one else was hurt, but Sally died right there, half-way home. Her father called me that evening.

He got right to it: "Hello, Danny. I'm sorry to have to tell you this. Sally's dead. She was killed in a car accident today."

My little sister Barrie picked up the phone on another extension just in time to hear him say this. I was upstairs; she was in the kitchen, far away. I could hear her scream, though, the bloodcurdling kind that cuts through every-thing. Sally's father hung up and I went into my bedroom. I still had one of her shirts in my closet, a half-used pack of her matches in the drawer of my bedside table. But she was not my girlfriend anymore, she hadn't been for a month or more, so it wasn't like my girlfriend died. It was like something else, but I didn't know what that was. The shock collapsed my throat. My sister told my parents and they rushed to my room, and I shivered until I cried. I wondered if I deserved to, though; the last thing I ever did to her was break her heart, after all. When I did cry—and I did, I'm almost embarrassed to say how much I cried—I felt like I was stealing somebody else's sorrow.

A week after Sally died, Holly and William returned to Birmingham. I thought they were just done with their travels, but later I found out they'd cut their trip short to be with me. My Age of Aquarius parents weren't helpful: they loved me very much, but my father wanted me to move past all my dark feelings as soon as possible, and my mother experienced feelings so deeply it made her nearly catatonic.

Holly and William had come to lure me back into the world. My sister Rangeley came back too. They took me to parties in the back of William's van. A month after Sally died, they took me to a bonfire out in the country. I brought my guitar. There were kegs and other guitars and I played songs with someone named Robert, who I'd never seen before and never saw again. Someone threw an old wicker chair on the fire and everybody cheered, including me. I had such a good time that for hours I forgot Sally was dead and didn't remember until we were on the way home, and I cried and cried. Forgetting her felt like a second betrayal. With the dull blade of a Swiss Army knife, I cut at my hands, drawing threads of blood, but never enough to make a solid drop. Pathetic.

Christmas came, New Year's, and in 1978 Holly and William left Alabama for good for Chapel Hill; Holly had gotten into graduate school in political science. I never asked her why she studied political science or what she planned to do with a degree in it, but in the end it didn't matter. Her arthritis overcame her. She never finished. Chapel Hill was perfect for William, though: there were so many rivers, so close by.

8 On Not Becoming a Writer

1979

MY FATHER HAD inherited a few acres of land from his parents on Smith Lake, outside of Cullman, in northern Alabama. Smith Lake is man-made; my grandparents had purchased the acreage before the lake even existed. I'd seen a grainy Super 8 film of the water rising as the Smith Dam filled the valley like a huge green bathtub, pine trees just peeking above the surface of the water. I was in the film, cradled in my mother's arms.

There was a small red cabin on the land, built on the side of a rocky orange-clay hill, roots of scrubby pine trees around it breaking through the dirt like bones. Perched on a stack of concrete blocks, rickety as an abandoned tree fort, the cabin was just as big as it needed to be: a small main room with a kitchen area (sink, hot plate, refrigerator), a bedroom, and a screened porch. No telephone, of course. It was the perfect place to write, to become a writer. The only problem was that I had never written a truly original story before, one that hadn't been stolen in style and structure and sometimes word for word from the writers I admired. It's said that good writers borrow and great writers steal, but I may have taken that dictum too far: I copied whole sentences from Walker Percy's *The Moviegoer* a couple of times. I didn't know what writing a real story entailed. But in the summer between my sophomore and junior year of college, this is where I went to do this thing I had never done, in the interests of making something, and making something of myself.

It didn't have much to do with making art, though. I was escaping. I was escaping my father, who wanted me to come work for him, eventually. I needed a reason not to, and if I became a writer, or believed that I *wanted* to be a writer, this might provide suitable cover, a reason why working for him would be a bad idea for both of us. This was to be at the import company that had bought us the big house. In his mind, I would become a traveling salesman—a world-traveling salesman, with a jet all my own, perhaps, long hours on the phone and in the office, wearing the clothes a businessman wears, making money. But I was more interested in *having* money than I was in actually making it. Champagne tastes, beer pocketbook.

"I wish I had raised you differently," he'd say. "Raised you to take over the business. But I didn't have the business then, and didn't until it was too late, and by then your mother had already got her claws into you."

Sometimes he'd laugh saying this, but other times he would scowl and shake his head. It was true: my mother often found ways to use us to perform acts of passive, and sometimes not so passive, aggression toward him. She championed every creative impulse I ever had, no matter how minor or artless, in no small part to put a wedge between me and my father, who felt the arts were self-indulgent navel-gazing, a sham, and just another way to leech off your family or the government because you were too lazy to get a real job. That did sound a little bit like me, actually.

Even my hair was the site of a tug-of-war between them. My mother wanted it as long as possible, and my father liked it neat and short. My mother got her way, and I was able to let it fall to my shoulders. When he'd get home from work my father would "confuse me" with my sisters. "Hello Holly," he'd say. "I mean Barrie. I mean Rangeley. Oh—wait—you're my son! I had no idea."

The summer of 1974, when I was fifteen, I had been out playing music with friends and, driving back late, we were stopped by police. In the top of pocket of my overalls I had secreted two joints. I tried to dispose of them before they got to the car, but the policemen saw me scrambling, and they found the joints, took us in, and told me a scary story: a girl my age who had dropped acid had hopped on top of their car and started "fucking the whirling blue light." They didn't arrest us, but they made us call our parents, who picked us up at the station at three in the morning.

"You really look the part," my father said. The next day my hair was shorn.

Still, I was his only son and he wanted me in his business. It was not what I wanted, though, and it wasn't what I wanted because (in part) it was not what I felt William would have wanted for me. Or: It was not how I would want to be seen through William's eyes. The truth is that I doubt he would have thought enough about it to care at all. He was my role model, but he didn't know that. He had no idea who he was to me. Sometimes I felt like I was stalking him, even when we lived four hundred miles apart.

So this is who I was, a boy whose dream, if it can be called a dream, was not to become a writer really, certainly not a novelist, but simply to become something *other*, demonstrably unique, amusing, living on the fringes. I was too passive, too lazy, intellectually unremarkable, ill-read, a talented dilettante really, though not without charm (the dilettante's secret weapon), whose goal was to somehow exist in the world without acquiring any official qualities or becoming a type. It all felt like a cliché, even to me then, and one of the worst clichés in the world was becoming a writer. But so was becoming anything, I thought.

It was so quiet on the lake that summer that you could hear a bug die. I had brought my Brother typewriter, an AM/FM radio, gin, tonic, cigarettes, a slim cardboard box of onion-skin paper—somehow, I thought that would help—and my dog, Orsin, an English bulldog. He sat in his own chair at the table, slept in the bed at my feet. I also brought two books: The Modern Library edition of *Ulysses* and a book that explained *Ulysses*, chapter by chapter: *James Joyce's* Ulysses: *Critical Essays*. The idea was that I would read a chapter from the novel, and then a chapter from the book explaining to me what I had just read.

It was a hot, rainless summer. I smoked pot and drank gin and watched the lake evaporate. By the end of summer, a quarter of the lake was gone, and the wooden dock was resting on the rocky shore. I didn't read much of *Ulysses*. The page where I stopped is still marked by the bookmark a girlfriend had given me, a heart made of thin silver. "Blazes Boylan looked in her blouse with more favour, the stalk of the red flower between his smiling teeth." That was the last sentence of *Ulysses* I read. The book explaining *Ulysses* fared even worse. I read the first chapter, wishing I'd brought a third book with me, explaining how to read the book about how to read *Ulysses*. I didn't write much. Writing was hard. The gin and tonics came earlier and earlier every day. My mother visited and brought me a picnic basket. I took day trips into town to shop and visit my great aunts and uncles. I waterskied. A family friend visited; he was just passing by. He was ten years older than I was, also from Alabama, and actually a working writer himself, a magazine writer, in New York City. His wife reviewed books. They lived in a loft on the Bowery. That sounded like a dream to me.

I fried up some bologna sandwiches for us. He asked after Holly and William, and I told him they'd moved to Chapel Hill, and William was building a house he'd designed, mapping rivers, clearing land lousy with copperheads.

"He doesn't kill them," I said. "He picks them up bare-handed and moves them to the creek. Which scares the shit out of me. Then does his writing and drawing, reading and all that. William," I said, "is a Renaissance man."

He laughed. "I don't *think* so," he said. "I mean, when you think of what a Renaissance man really was. In comparison I think you could say that William is . . . handy."

This was stunning to me, that he would feel differently, that anyone could deny William's place in the world. So condescending, I thought.

Still, he was a writer, and I was not, and after the bologna sandwiches he drove away into his romantic writing life while my days on the lake were only getting longer. Every word I typed on my onionskin paper felt like it had been pried from my fingers with pliers, even the words *a* and *the*. Clearly, I realized, I was no writer. At least I was learning what I wasn't, an important lesson in and of itself. So by process of elimination—not a banjo player, not a writer—I was a businessman, like it or not. I would turn myself in to my father after college to begin serving my life sentence.

I still needed to do something to make this summer feel worthwhile. I drove to town and bought a quart of sunshine yellow paint and started to paint the bedroom, but only painted one wall before I gave up. Apparently I was not much of a painter, either.

Then I had an idea. After six weeks of swimming in the lake and gin, I called William and asked if he could tell me how to build a table. Even if I couldn't write, my thinking went, I could make something to write *on*.

Of course he could. But not over the phone. He would send me directions.

Days later it came: a drawing of what he called the Platonic Table.

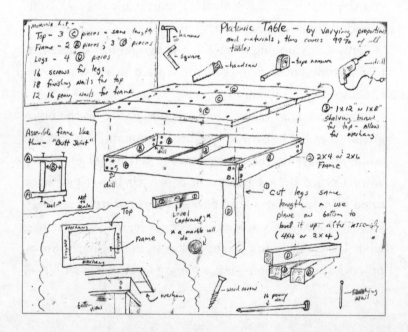

The illustration included every tool I would need, every piece of wood, every screw, every nail. Where to put them and when, from every angle. It must have taken him hours to draw.

So I built a table. Not a good table, not a Platonic Table. But it was a better thing than anything else I made that summer, and it affirmed a connection, however tenuous, with William. I did what he would have done, albeit poorly. There was hope for me yet. Orsin and I would sit in our chairs and eat our breakfast, lunch, and dinner on it. But I had to be careful: it tilted so far to one side that my gin and tonic tipped over if I set it down too close to the edge. But that was the difference between William and me: I never got as close to the edge as he did. I wasn't that brave, or talented. William was all in, though, all the time, and while I couldn't be that person, I was drawn to him because he could. Our different approaches to the edge played out conspicuously in our separate relationships with one extraordinary person, Edgar Hitchcock.

Edgar had originally been William and Holly's friend before he became mine, and William's best friend, in fact. I'd known Edgar for a while, but just as Holly's little brother; in 1977, however, after Sally died and William and Holly were gone on their excursions, he and I started meeting up once or twice a week. He was the kindest man I had ever met, so smart, funny, and loving. He had scoliosis, a serious curvature of the spine, and so his shoulders were lopsided, with one shoulder blade more prominent than the other, and his hips were uneven. His pants hung at a loose, sloping angle; his legs were so thin they looked lost inside them. He was five seven, wore tinted aviator sunglasses, Hawaiian shirts, and he carried a leather man-bag long before man-bags were cool. He had a wry smile, a sharp wit, a playful, devious cackle. The curvature at the top of his spine presented itself as a hump. A small hump. The first time you met him you would notice it, but it would turn out to be the least important thing about him, and once you knew him for more than five minutes you'd forget about it altogether.

When he was thirteen years old he'd endured an eight-hour surgery on his back. The surgery was to insert an implant—called a Harrington rod—meant to provide stability, preventing further curvature of the spine. The Harrington rod was fitted with hooks at both ends and a ratchet. The hooks were secured onto the vertebra, and then the vertebra was fused. It was like getting a new metal spine—a stainless steel supporting rod. It didn't correct the curve of his spine but supported it from curving further and crushing his lungs, which was how his brother Malcolm, who was born with the same condition, had died. Malcolm had been too fragile for the operation. Although the surgery saved Edgar's life, he'd felt like it was a temporary reprieve, as if his days were numbered, and if that was the case, he was going to live them on the edge. He was going to tempt the worst sort of fate. And thus he became a drug dealer, over time becoming a major source of cocaine in Birmingham. He made trips to southern Florida a few times a year with a couple of friends and a courier, buying cocaine from Colombians in hotel rooms, surrounded by drugs, cash, and machine guns. He would drive back up to Birmingham, cut it up and sell it. Then he would take some time for himself and write a short story or two. I have some of them, detective stories mostly, written in the hard-boiled style.

This was Edgar: small and fragile and smart, but with a death wish. Why would he and William be so close? If William was an Adonis, Edgar was a court jester. Years would pass before I would figure it out, that they were twins, fun-house mirror twins. Because William, too, was a fool for danger and, I would learn, led a secret life, and, like Edgar, thought his time here was going to be short.

Edgar was in the restaurant business, the floor manager for a popular Southside bar called Dugan's, and later part owner of Birmingham's first gourmet pizza joint, Cosmo's. But he thrived on the rush of his side hustle. I saw him about once a week or so, usually at his place, in Southside. In one corner of his living room was a large green plant, and in another a life-size cardboard facsimile of Humphrey Bogart, in a brown suit, wearing a fedora, smoking a cigarette and looking at you, kid. There was the glass-topped coffee table, standard for a coke dealer, and a chessboard to one side of it, where a game was always ongoing, waiting for the other guy's move.

Edgar was the first person I knew who actually spent time writing and talking about writing and writers. Hemingway, Hammett, Chandler, Vonnegut, and someone new we had both just discovered, Raymond Carver. He was the first person outside of my family I told I might want to be a writer one day.

We'd talk about books and movies and Holly and William, while he cut lines on the glass table.

"Are you sure this is okay?" he'd ask me from time to time, as if I needed permission to buy coke from him. I assured him that it was. My parents loved Edgar, too, though I don't think they would have given me the go-ahead on this.

One night, we exchanged short stories. Mine was a high schooler's knockoff of a Raymond Carver story. It was about a couple in an apartment building having sex while the lonely guy who lived below them listened longingly; his was the beginning of a novella, *Urban Birds*. I loved Edgar's style, his dialogue: "Don't get too sloppy on me. Or maudlin. I hate maudlin." "Your friend Gary was bent like a hairpin, and a lot of people involved in this thing know it because they're bent too."

Edgar wrote more letters than stories, though, beautiful letters to me full of wisecracks and wisdom. One of them I read and reread years after receiving it, after I sent him a story and, in the same letter, told him I was thinking about going to work for my father. He told me what a mistake that might be.

I tried to warn you . . . You've no doubt made the
same observatory [sic] that most writers are better
left in the figurative or literal closet. I complicate
matters for you and say (for what it's worth) that
you alas poor boy are not one of them. The demon
is free. Free to wreak havoc upon yon suspecting
world that must be wrought by some damned soul
with nothing to look forward to but impossible
tasks and lonely vigils on dark nights with a cold
wind humming soprano dirges in your unresisting
ear. Better get a scarf and a bottle of scotch. Better
read <u>Metamorphosis</u> by Kafka too. He's talking
about being a writer in that story. Did you know?
Apparently it makes him feel like a giant roach. We
have so much to look forward to.

I know that's a long time to go on about Edgar. I'm
only introducing him now, a little early, because I loved
him and because he helped me survive and because he
was like William in so many ways—they were spiritual
doppelgängers—and I feel like I have to hurry up and tell
you that. He's going to die soon, and his death will mark
the beginning of the end of this story. After Edgar, William
won't be far behind.

Raccoon Empire

"Someday son, this will all be yours..."

9 Waiting for My Father to Land

1980

THAT FALL, INSTEAD of returning to Emory University, where I'd spent my first two years of college, I transferred to the University of North Carolina at Chapel Hill. I'd never been on the UNC campus or spoken a word to anyone who went there. But Holly and William were living in Chapel Hill, and it was the only place I wanted to be. I took a creative writing class. I wrote a story, shyly under a pseudonym, T. Corolla, after my car, and it was published in *Cellar Door*, the undergraduate literary magazine. Orsin and I lived in a basement apartment that flooded when it rained. But most of my time was spent at the little cinder-block house where Holly and William lived.

I began a clandestine relationship with one of their friends. She was eight years older than me. We slept together all the time, but didn't go out in public together very much, and wouldn't speak to each other at parties, because she was embarrassed by how much younger I was. One night after getting dinner, she was driving me back to my basement apartment and said, "I'm guessing it's okay if I come in for a while."

She really didn't have to ask. It was expected that she would "come in for a while," because this was who we were together: wet kisses and a quick turnaround. Then we'd smoke the way they do in the movies.

"Actually," I said. "Not tonight. I have a lot of homework. Reading, and a test."

She slowed the car as we drove up the steep and busy road that led to my apartment.

"Homework? Seriously?"

"I'll have to get right to work."

She wouldn't even look at me. Halfway up the hill, my apartment still half a mile away, she stopped the car. "Get out," she said.

Cars blew by, honking in the passing lane.

"You're kidding," I said.

"Do I look like I'm kidding?"

She finally turned to me. I stared her down and then she stared me down and then I got out of the car. She drove away and I crossed the street in heavy traffic and walked up the road to my dark, damp basement home, where Orsin was waiting.

I didn't have homework. But I could not tell her the awful truth: that I wanted to write a story.

Another year passed. I had published a story in an undergraduate magazine, but whatever was supposed to happen next had not. My father called with an offer: work for his business in Japan, no strings attached, see if it suited me. It was impossible to refuse: a life in Japan, with no commitment beyond my stay there. I'd come to the end of my senior year and discovered I didn't have the credits to graduate: I had skipped the science and math requirements. No matter. My father hadn't graduated from college, my mother hadn't graduated from college, and most important, William hadn't even graduated from high school. I was in good company. So I moved to Japan. Holly and William took Orsin, while I spent the next two years in Nagoya, Kagoshima, and Yokkaichi, in factories and offices all over the country, learning my father's business from the ground up.

There were not a lot of foreigners, *gaijin* we were called, where I lived. I was a tall, white celebrity wherever I went, even when I worked at a massive factory stapling boxes shut for eight hours a day.

I missed home, I missed my dog. I lived for the mail. I begged for letters. William wrote me more than anyone else. He even sent me a mixtape. He told me about Orsin's new favorite bone, a cow's tibia William had found out West. It was a bone that had once been part of a "kinetic sculpture" he'd made, bones hung by a rawhide strip, slowly rotting in the woods. He shared ideas he was working on for cartoons: Old Testament jokes for a stand-up comedian performing at the Noah's Ark Dinner Theater. Jokes like, "Last time I was here it was raining cats and frogs!"

It fell to William to write me when Orsin died. He'd had an aneurysm, which blew out in his chest.

"We buried him yesterday evening down by the creek," William wrote, the creek where, twenty-five years later, Holly would want me to scatter her ashes with William's, "and we came back to the house and looked at old pictures of our Orsin, which was fun . . . Well, I hope you're okay . . ."

I hope you're okay. I could almost hear the words battling through his tight-lipped machismo. It was the closest he ever got to sharing a feeling like that. It was great, but it was also like being hugged by someone without any arms.

In October 1983, my father came to visit. Many Japanese homes were designed in a half-Western, half-Japanese style: to the left as you entered was a traditional Japanese living room, a tatami mat and low wooden table, maybe a small simple vase. To the right was a room with a sofa, chairs, and a television, carpeted with a dense, low-pile weave, ersatz art on the walls.

My father and I sat to the right and drank and smoked Japanese cigarettes. Earlier that evening we'd walked down the block for some sushi and sake. I told him about my girlfriend, Teruko, who wanted to go back to America with me. We stayed up late, dressed in our yukatas, drinking cognac and listening to Ella Fitzgerald. We agreed that "Begin the Beguine" was not our favorite song by Ella, although Cole Porter was the best songwriter who ever lived.

By eleven we were drunk, loopy, digging on the tunes and Japan and this remarkable moment, the luck and hard work that had brought us here, although in truth it was not due to my hard work at all. I was just riding his wave.

He waited until almost midnight: "So I know I said there would be no strings," he said.

"Right."

"And there aren't any. But I have to make some decisions soon, about where I want the business to go. I need to know."

"Know."

"If you're signing on or not."

"That sounds like a string."

"It's a development. I have to know. If I go left it's one thing and if I go right it's another. You know, and I mean this—I think you can do this job. People like you. Everybody here likes you. You're well liked. You're doing great. And you like it, right?"

When you're drunk and your father is drunk and it's closing in on midnight, you have to be careful what you say. "I do," I said. But what I meant was I was having fun living in Japan eating sushi and drinking sake and cognac and smoking Peace cigarettes and hanging out with my Japanese girlfriend.

Sometimes my father likened himself to Philip II of Macedonia, and me to Alexander the Great. Philip, he said, had laid all the groundwork for everything that Alexander did—conquer the world, that is—but got almost none of the credit. My dad would be fine with that, though, he said, because if not for Alexander no one would have remembered Philip at all.

But I knew the job wasn't for me, even though I didn't know what *was* for me. I hadn't written a word of fiction in a year and a half, only letters back home and a few notes toward stories I might write one day, if one day I ever wrote. One idea I have yet to tackle: *Has there been anything written about Darius and the Persians' attack on Athens from their point of view? Who to ask?*

My father would not take his eyes off me. "So?"

"No," I said. "I mean, god, thank you, for everything. But I just don't see myself doing this, or doing it very well if I did. I don't think I'm good at it, really, but even if I were—"

"Even if you were, what?"

"Good at it. Even if I were good at it, I'm not sure that I would like it," I said. "That I would be happy."

He gave me his slit-eyed death stare for what felt like a thousand years. "Happiness. Who said anything about happiness? And you're going to do what instead?"

I couldn't say what I was going to do instead. It was too

embarrassing. I might as well have said I wanted to become an astronaut, for all the sense it made.

"*Write?*" he asked, as if it were the most ridiculous alternative to a life in business that he could think of. It was ridiculous, though. It didn't make even a little sense. I had shown no propensity or capacity for it. What was I thinking?

But I kind of nodded. Or maybe I just looked away. Ella wasn't singing anymore. Japan felt like a very quiet country right then.

"Then go home," he said. "No reason for you to be here now."

And he went to bed.

I did go home a few months later. I returned to Chapel Hill. Back in the States, my father wouldn't speak to me. I left messages for him at his office, called him at home. Nothing. When he accidentally picked up, he said he couldn't talk, because he was "really, really busy here, Son." I got it: he had built his business from nothing, made this incredible thing, and his son had decided to pass, and for what? *To become a writer.* For all the writing I'd done in my life up to that point, I could have just as easily set my sights on becoming a hot air balloonist or a tap dancer.

After three months in Chapel Hill, typing the terrible stories I sent to the *New Yorker* and *Harper's* and the *Atlantic* while working in a bookstore, I drove to Birmingham to see my father. He had a small private jet at the time. He was so proud of it, this boy from Cullman, Alabama, who left the little town where he'd been raised with hopes of greater things. He was rightly proud. It was an amazing story. He was a big fish now and he had done it all on his own, just by working hard and being a little bit smarter than "the other guy." There was always *the other guy* in his stories, the guy who was out there wanting the same thing you wanted, and who might take it from you if you didn't work twice as hard as he did. My father had worked twice as hard. I'd inherited some of that ethic from him, at least. When he told me he was getting a jet, it had seemed preposterous but now that he had, it had been folded into our lives as if it were a new lawn chair. I'd been on it a couple of times. It even had a telephone in it, and in 1983 that was *wild*. I'd called my mother from 20,000 feet. He loved to fly us around. He'd flown me up to Chapel Hill when I was in school there, taken me and my friends to Florida, flown our family to the Caribbean.

He was out of town when I got to Birmingham. I hung out at my mother's for a while, then I called his office to find out when he'd be flying in, and they told me, and I drove to the airport and parked behind the hangar he shared with the fabulously rich. I walked out on the tarmac and sat down. Planes flew in and out of the clouds. The sun warmed the cracked and buckling concrete. It warmed me, too. I lay on my back and looked at the sky and waited for my father to land.

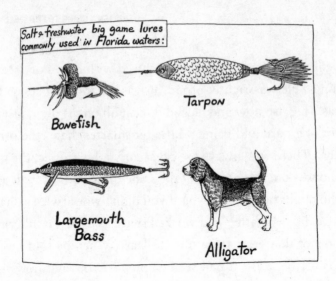

Salt & freshwater big game lures commonly used in Florida waters:

Bonefish

Tarpon

Largemouth Bass

Alligator

10 A Day Not Spent Fishing Is a Day Lost Forever
1984

SOON AFTER I'D returned from Japan, William took me fishing.

The desire to write fiction—the reason I had given for not working for my father—was in itself a fiction. I had no stories I wanted to write, no goals. Though I had written stories and even had one published(!), I found that, now that I was a year out of school, everything I'd learned had been forgotten. Every book I'd ever read, every idea, whatever writing skills I'd developed—it was as if none of it had ever happened. I didn't even know how to set up the typewriter so it would automatically indent, and so my first stories, no matter how many pages they were, were all one paragraph long.

I had everything I needed to become a writer except for an interesting life to draw from. Stories don't just happen; even the most outlandish of them begin with an experience, or an experience you've borrowed from a neighbor or a friend. But nothing had ever happened to me worth writing about. So I looked to William for help with that, and he provided it.

William, whose first book of river maps had been collected and published in 1981, was the first person I ever knew who wrote a real book—a book that *became* a book, words and images on a page that were printed, bound, and sold. This was so important to me—knowing someone who had taken an idea, dressed it up, and sent it out into the world. The way we first see books is as beautiful parcels of words in cloth covers, unmarred, perfect, without a drop of sweat anywhere on them, not a single torn or crumpled page. No blood. There was no way the tangled and tortured process of actual writing, the days and nights of minor triumphs and major defeats, could ever add up to something as beautiful as a book. But to be able to watch someone do it—someone I actually knew—changed all that. *If he could do it, why couldn't I?* When I'd visit Holly and William at their home, he would often be bent over his light table, tracing the penciled lines of his drawings in ink, every detail of every rock and rapid, pouring over his character's expressions—the paddlers and their girlfriends—scene, character, conflict. Watching him gave me permission to begin writing in 1984, and also was the reason that the first writing desk I bought was a drafting table.

But there was even more I wanted him to teach me.

I wanted him to teach me how to fish.

He, of course, liked nothing more.

I was twenty-four and I'd never been fishing in my life. My father had never taken me fishing and that was fine with me. But now that I was a man and wanting to be a writer and needing to understand what happened when you killed things, I felt like I was missing something valuable, and so I turned to William to show me what it was.

William would have shown me how to do anything I asked him to. He would have made an amazing father himself. Nieces and nephews, the neighbor's kids, they all loved him, and not just because he made a camp for them in his backyard—with a climbing wall and a tree house and a mesh tent to spider-walk over—but because he saw the world through their eyes. He saw the world as a place for homemade adventure.

Fishing was integral to the idea of being the writer I was now ambitious to become. Not all the writers I admired fished, of course. Flannery O'Conner may have, Salinger, probably not. I can't imagine Kafka fishing; Nabokov captured butterflies. But as a Southern writer, which is what I was or what I would likely become once I wrote anything, fishing was a *requirement*. Up until that point, for most of the almost quarter of a century I'd been alive, I had stayed indoors, preferring hot showers, soft pillows, and central air. But there was no story there. I was afraid that my desire to be a writer would not be commensurate with things to write about; I was afraid I would never have an opportunity to use the word *commensurate*. I remember wishing, honestly wishing, that I hadn't missed Vietnam, because there was so much great material there! *Going After Cacciato, Dispatches, The Things They Carried*. I loved those books. In Vietnam I would have had lot of friends who would have died, or parts of them would have been blown off, and maybe parts of me as well, and I would have watched as whole villages were razed and women and children sent fleeing into the forest. Dark and unspeakable tragedy upon tragedy. It would have scarred me, but at the end of the day I would have been okay enough, at home with my typewriter, writing about it. William had not gone to Nam either, but he had read a hundred books about it and maintained all of his life a weirdly intense and fiery hatred for Lt. William Calley, who perpetrated the massacre at My Lai.

William was the kind of man Hemingway would have liked, the kind of man who could be dropped into the middle of a jungle with no more than a half-chewed piece of bubble gum, a piece of dental floss, and the pop-top from a cola can and somehow still save your life.

I borrowed one of his fishing rods and we got up early and bought some night crawlers at a bait shop. Night crawlers are worms, worms as big as garter snakes, and you could buy a box of them for three dollars. We bought two boxes and headed out to the country where a friend of William's had a medium-sized pond stocked with bass and bream. We took the poles and night crawlers and an ice chest big enough to hold two six-packs. The plan was that when the six packs were gone we were done fishing whether we'd caught anything or not.

It was the kind of summer when it was never not unbearably hot except for a few seconds just before dawn. But as soon as the sun rose and there was a light over the dusty rain-starved pine-tree-mottled land, you felt seized by the heat, as if in the arms of a chain-smoking uncle you never really liked, all sweaty and pungent and sticky. Mosquitos traveled in cloudy gangs and attacked with the single-minded ferocity of hungry lions.

Why fishing, though? Why not hunting? He was expert with a bow and arrow, and with guns. He had an affection for guns and, same as everything else he cared for, knew a lot about them. He had quite a few of them that I'd only seen once. William and Holly's bathroom was expansive. It was one long room, like a railroad car, separated by sliding wooden doors. One room was the actual bathroom, the second was a changing room, and the third was where they kept the washer and dryer.

One summer day I was visiting, swimming in their pool.

"I was hoping I could borrow a towel," I said.

William took me to the changing room where the towels were hanging from hooks on a wall. I saw, as I took one that was only slightly damp, an almost imperceptible crack in the wall.

"Look at this," I said, as if I might be showing him something he wouldn't already have known about. He kept a keen eye on every nook and cranny of the little kingdom he had created.

"Oh that," he said. "Yeah."

He pulled on one of the hooks, and the wall moved. It opened. It wasn't a wall at all but a "fake" wall he'd inserted during construction. Behind it was a display of shotguns, handguns, rifles, and scary-looking knives and machetes. He kept nunchucks back there, too, and bows and arrows.

"Just in case," he said. "For the end times." He chuckled, making fun of the kind of people who believed in that sort of thing, even though, you know, he kind of believed in that sort of thing.

He lived for desperate moments, for the most exceptional emergencies in which to perform. What more exceptional emergency was there than the end of days?

The man who owned the pond we were fishing was named Rod Farb. Rod was thirty-five, and a deep-sea diver. He'd explored the bottom of the Atlantic Ocean off the coast of North Carolina looking for ancient shipwrecks, and he had found some, too, and he wrote books about that. He was a big man with long black hair and a grand mustache in the style favored by Mongol invaders, and he wore the kind of glasses that turned dark in the sun. He seemed to me to exist in the same world William did, full of brilliance and arcane knowledge. They were men who saw the world

as something to be fathomed through direct experience—
something I wanted, too, but I wanted to have it without
actually having to experience it *that* much. I wanted access
to it through hanging out with people who did experience
it, and then writing about the things they did.

Rod never fished with us, but after the third or fourth
time out there, he joined us for a cigarette.

"William told me you were a writer."

"Not really," I said. "Not yet. I'm learning. Giving it a
shot."

He nodded. I felt him take my estimation behind his
dark glasses.

"I want to show you something," he said, and gestured
for me and William to follow.

He took us about twenty yards away from the pond and
we edged through a copse of thick pine until we came to a
clearing and a large metal cage, about twenty feet square.
Inside the cage was a Bengal tiger, all golden brown with
slashing black stripes. She lay there, looking at us with her
I'm-Not-Kidding-I-Will-Eat-You eyes. Then she stood and
paced from one end of the cage to the other, impatiently, as
if she were on a platform waiting for a train.

"Can you go in?" I said.

"In the cage? I can," he said. "But just me. Anybody else
and she'd rip them apart. Want to give it a shot?" His smile
was almost hostile, almost as if he would have let me if I'd
taken him up on it.

"No thanks," I said.

"I didn't think so," he said, and Rod and William laughed.

I don't know how he got the tiger, or where it came from, or if it was even legal to have it there. But just a few minutes ago I had been fishing and then I'd been taken behind a scrim of green and now here we were and it was so random, as if anything could have been hiding behind the pine trees, anything at all, but today it just happened to be a tiger.

We left the beast and returned to the pond, and drank beer, and fished.

We caught a few. Most of them we threw back because they were so small. But I hauled in a bass that weighed over a pound and William taught me how to kill it, descale it, and gut it right there. A fish skull is so fragile. All you have to do is lop it once or twice with a rock or a stick or knock it against a hard piece of wood like a dock, and the fish will be dead. William used the knife he always had with him and showed me how to shave off its scales, and how to slit the underbelly and remove everything inside until it was hollow, just bones and meat. Other than ants and grasshoppers, this fish was the first living being I had ever killed. Later we would take it to his house and cook it up. It was good and fine and true, as someone might say.

Yes, I needed more of this in my fiction. More guts, more death, fewer broken hearts and talking dogs. I was so bored with myself and despairing of ever writing anything worth reading. This half-acre pond was where stories were born, I thought, in the dark and unexplored forest around it, on the reefs where ships sank, with the wild animal hidden behind the pines. I needed to be more like William, like Rod. I needed to get in the cage with the tiger.

In 2003, Rod Farb murdered his wife, her daughter, and a friend of his wife's who had come there to protect her. Then he killed himself. All this at the house by the pond where William and I had gone fishing. Rod had a drinking problem, they said. In 2000 he'd been charged with flying while impaired, when he crashed a plane. But news reports said "there was not a lot in Farb's background" to suggest why he'd killed three people before killing himself, and no one, including one of his stepsons, has been able to shed a light on it. The tiger was gone long before this happened, but why he got rid of it, and where it went, I don't know.

11 A White Christmas

WILLIAM AND I would drive in tandem from Chapel Hill to Birmingham, for Christmas, then drive the eight hours back. We did this year after year. Sometimes Holly would stay a little longer and fly back later. Before leaving Birmingham, we'd get a gram of coke from Edgar—a Christmas present. We'd take turns holding it. We could have split it up but if the worst happened and one of us was busted the other could go for help. William had thought this through.

We had CB radios. We'd find a channel all our own and chatter, the lead car miles ahead watching for speed traps.

Smokie at mile marker 177, over.

That's a 10-4, over.

The lead car had the coke. An hour into the trip we'd make the first exchange.

The next rest stop, over.

Copy that, over.

Then, minutes later: *Second one down from the door, over,* he'd say. William loved codes. He could have been a secret agent or a detective, I thought.

I'd pull into the rest stop. William would be long gone. In the second stall from the door, behind the tank, he would have taped the bindle. I'd retrieve it, do a line sitting on the john. Eventually I'd pass him, becoming the lead car, and would perform the same exchange an hour later. This is how we'd drive through Georgia, South Carolina, and home to Chapel Hill. By the time we got back it would all be gone, and Christmas was officially over.

I loved my life with William.

In the summers in the eighties we'd ride our mountain bikes into downtown Chapel Hill, thumping down flights of concrete stairs on campus, on sidewalks in front of the Varsity Theater, in and out of traffic, as free as anybody was anywhere, as free as anyone ever had been. Eventually, we'd end up at the Cave, a bar in the basement of a building. The chairs were hard and uncomfortable, the lighting was bad, it was poorly ventilated, everybody smoked. There was an old jukebox featuring scratched-up 45s, of Otis Redding singing "(Sittin' on) the Dock of the Bay," of "Yellow Submarine" and the Ramones, and yet no matter how loud it got, you could still hear the crack of a cue ball crashing above the felt. There was an ancient black payphone with a rotary dial, with the number of a cab service scrawled on the wall. The front door was at the bottom of a steep grade of worn concrete stairs, which always seemed damp. The back entrance was a door off an unlit gravel parking lot, where even a short man had to stoop to enter. This is where we'd park our bikes—no locks, just leaned them against the wall—and play pool for hours.

Holly rarely came. There was nothing for her to do, no comfortable place for her to sit, and it wasn't bright enough to read. It was just the two of us. Surely this is where we became true friends. These nights. A little brother no longer, I could do everything he could do, and we could do it together. Riding bikes, smoking cigarettes, playing pool, drinking cheap beer: these were the rituals that brought us close. We never said as much—ever. We never would.

There were the songs we listened to, and bands, and there were specific sounds we were drawn to—loud, angry and playful at the same time. The singer-songwriters of the 1970s were torture for us. Anyone who could write and sing about their inner demons and broken hearts made him snarl and I snarled along with him. If Jackson Browne, Joni Mitchell, and Crosby, Stills and Nash walked into a bar we were in, we would have walked out.

The Ramones, Captain Beefheart, the Go-Go's, the Rolling Stones (*not* the Beatles), Siouxsie and the Banshees, the Psychedelic Furs, Concrete Blonde, Alice Cooper, the B-52's, Devo, the Cars, Holly and the Italians ("Tell That Girl to Shut Up"), Frank Zappa, the Hampton Grease Band, the Modern Lovers, Pet Shop Boys, the Pretenders, Romeo Void, the Vapors, the Beastie Boys and, for Holly, Leon Russell ("A Song For You"). William made mixtapes for the cassette player in his van and at stoplights he'd match the beat of the song with his hands on the steering wheel, drumming, the music up too loud to talk. He would never sing along. The music we liked was tough, hard-edged, with as little naked, tear-stained emotion in it as possible. No tear stains, please. My memories of these days, these years, are so vivid, but no stories are being told. The beginnings, middles, and ends don't fit together. I remember bits and pieces of a night, of an adventure. The two of us on our way to campus, windows down, on our way to the gentleman's club that time, biking to Italian Pizzeria III for a slice. Watching a band at Cat's Cradle. Smoking, chewing Nicorette, both at the same time. My memories are like scratchy, unfocused surveillance photos of my own life. So much must have happened that I can't remember enough to know what I've forgotten.

But always there was music and musicians. I remember them all. And more than any of the others, and maybe more than any of them put together, there was Warren Zevon, especially his LP *Excitable Boy*. "Werewolves of London," "Excitable Boy," "Roland the Headless Thompson Gunner"—about a mercenary, "a warrior," who, even after his head is blown off, continues on a revenge quest for those who killed him—was a very real part of William's brain, his worldview, his sense of self, and the soundtrack to our lives back then. *They can still see his headless body stalking through the night.*

The one song that seemed to break all the rules with its openness to sharing the deeply felt anguish of existence was "The Beast in Me," by Nick Lowe. The quiet emotional torment of the singer, who understands his condition but also realizes there is absolutely nothing he can do about it, is so deep and real. It's as if Dr. Jekyll wrote a song about Mr. Hyde. William had this on a mixtape, maybe on more than one. It spoke to him in ways I wouldn't understand for decades. "The beast in me / Is caged by frail and fragile bars."

I thought it spoke to me, too. But I wondered, and I still wonder, how much of it was me and how much of it was me trying to be William. To appear to be the kind of man who is on the side of the angels most, but not all, of the time; who shows no vulnerability because he is so vulnerable; who carries around some dark secret that's so sharp it can't be touched, and so heavy it can't be moved. And I thought back to the day we saw the tiger by the pond where we were fishing. I asked Rod if I could get in the cage with it, and William and Rod laughed—at me, I thought at the time. But now I think they laughed because here was this kid wanting to get in a cage, right in front of these two grown men who would have liked nothing better than to get out.

12 Renaissance Man in a Neoprene Suit

I see white water, climbing, fishing etc not only as
athletic pursuits but a way of being in the picture, a
part of the gestalt. Sitting in a beauty spot, I'm aware
of myself sitting, looking out of my "eye windows."
A disconnect. On a bike or a rope or in a boat you're
a physical part of the picture and (depending on
the level of concentration/fear) objectively involved
(unity) with the environment.   —William Nealy, 1989

THIS SHOULD BE the easiest chapter in the book to write, but
it's not. It's one of the hardest, even though—or maybe
because—it's where all the good things happen. I want it to
be the last chapter, where I somehow eke out that rare and

elusive happy ending. But I know how this is going to end, no matter how many of his dreams come true. That's why all the applause he gets, all the kudos— the public recognition an artist can never count on but can only hope for—comes off as sort of flat to me, and maybe why it didn't inspire or delight him very much either: I think he knew how it was going to end as well. It's supposed to be the chapter of the victory lap, the rising crescendo of the audience going wild, a montage of pure joy, the part of the story where you realize that it's all been worth it. This is supposed to be his moment.

Ever since moving from Alabama to North Carolina in the early 1980s, William's life had become busy and layered. He'd built the sprawling house in the woods of Hillsborough with the help of friends, clearing the forest, thinning out the copperheads. It was a long house, just one story, built for the day when Holly would no longer be able to take the stairs. They had a few neighbors, three or four houses hidden in the woods. When it snowed, William plowed; when the bridge at the bottom of the hill flooded, he ferried his neighbors across in his van; when a tree fell, he was the one who cut it up with a chainsaw.

He was a busy man. He was busy taking care of Holly, of his dogs, pigs, house, copperheads, and turtles, busy fixing and building things for people, including me. He was out on the river as often as he possibly could be. A police scanner sat on his bedside table, and he listened to it all the time, ready to help strangers through their disasters. There were books that needed reading, movies that needed watching. But at the same time William was checking items off his list of things to do. He loved to make lists: 1. *Decide what I will be—Adventurer, Cartoonist, Artist, Writer.*

By the eighties he was exactly that. He was an artist, a cartoonist, an adventurer. He was a writer—even a cartographer: this was his special gift. He drew meticulous cartoon-laden river maps that pointed out problematic rapids and things you might see along the shoreline and how you might feel at every juncture. Looking at one, you felt as if he'd memorized every rock, rapid, and eddy. Later his creations would expand to include rock climbing, mountain biking, skiing, even inline skating. His playful, edgy style finally found its natural genre, a genre that didn't exist before he created it. And like so many great concepts, it happened almost by accident.

William was twenty-five when he and Holly had moved to Chapel Hill. He was unemployed. He'd had a few cartoons published in random outdoor magazines, one in *Outside* magazine, for which they paid him six dollars. He needed a job, but he knew he couldn't handle a "real" one. He had never been suited to wearing a suit, to living and working in what he called the "mainstream culture." But soon there would be no way to avoid it: they were living in a cinder-block house, paying rent with Holly's teaching stipend and handouts from my father.

Forestalling this eventuality for as long as he possibly could, he finally got a job in a tiny paddle shop in Durham, renting canoes on the Haw River. "I spent so much time giv-ing directions to the put-in and drawing diagrams of rapids on scraps of paper that I finally just drew a big poster of the river. It was a river caricature with prototypical boater wipe-out cartoons."

They put it out for sale at the shop, and by the end of that paddling season he'd sold over one hundred maps. If he drew a map for a river that had real viability, he could possibly make a living doing this. The closest commercially rafted river to Chapel Hill is called the Nantahala, and it's about an hour southwest of Asheville. He had kayaked it many times. "I knew every rock and riffle," he wrote. (A riffle, I would learn, is a shallow place in a river where the water flows past rocks.)

He drew the map on spec. On the way home for Christmas, he and Holly stopped at the outpost on the Nantahala River and, without an appointment, took it to the outdoor center. William hoped someone would at least look at it and maybe like the map enough to order a few dozen, on consignment; that would be something, a start.

He showed the map to John Barber, who was running the place.

"His hair was pretty long and he had on dark glasses," Barber remembered. He would later become one of William's best friends. "He kind of had that artsy bohemian look."

But Barber liked what he saw. He ordered a thousand. This is the map that showed William how he might be able to bring all the things he loved—his life as an artist and his life as an adventurer, or a "fun hog," as he put it—together at last. William created his own company, Class Seven River Maps ("Class Six" is the designation for the most hazardous river rapid; Class Seven is practically suicidal) and began mapping all the major rivers of the Southeast. By 1981 he'd mapped ten southeastern rivers, distributing them on his own, outpost to outpost. Not long after this, a publisher named Bob Sehlinger asked if William would be interested in doing a book. "I literally slid down the wall onto the floor, knocking over a paddle display."

"His maps were totally original," Bob says. "He had a singular sense of humor and his ability to explain paddling and complicated hydrology in art form was singular. There was nothing like it out there and there hasn't been anything like it since."

His first book, *Whitewater Home Companion*, was published in 1981 by Menasha Ridge Press, a new company founded by Holly, William, and Bob and financed, in the beginning, by my father. William would write and illustrate ten books, including *Kayak: A Manual* in 1986, *The Mountain Bike Way of Knowledge* in 1990, and *Inline!* Each of them, he wrote, was "a memoir, a thesis of my learning." His last book, in 2000, was one that every writer dreams of, a Best Of: *The Nealy Way of Knowledge: Twenty Years of Extreme Cartoons.*

"His books arose from his own learning curve," Bob says. "His learning curve in paddling, his learning curve in skiing, his learning curve in inline skating. He would learn these things and become proficient, and then be able to articulate what and how he learned through his art in the books."

The fantastical world William yearned for, one where he could make his art on his own terms, outside of the mainstream culture, had been willed into existence. And as I watched his life unfold like this, I wondered, in brief moments of what felt like pointless reverie, if I could do the same.

Today the Nantahala Outdoor Center—the NOC—is a huge enterprise, and one of the most popular river runs in the country. In an office near the canoe repair shop, there's an extensive archive of William's original drawings, cartoons, and maps. There are over a thousand individual entries, some of them notebooks full of text and drawings, T-shirt designs: a mammoth collection. It's here you can see the scope of his work. In this room, surrounded by it all, I felt like I was walking into his mind.

The maps themselves, printed in their entirety, are each over three feet long. But it's the details that astound. It's more than just a charming illustration: every rock he drew was of an actual rock that a kayaker or canoeist would encounter; arrows indicated the ideal path through the river; even the presence of micro-eddies (circular movements of water, counter to the main current, causing a small whirlpool) is helpfully indicated. Then there's the photographer, the sunbather, the hapless tuber screaming for help—there was something interesting, educational, or amusing in every square inch of it. Here's a very small section from the Nantahala map.

And this:

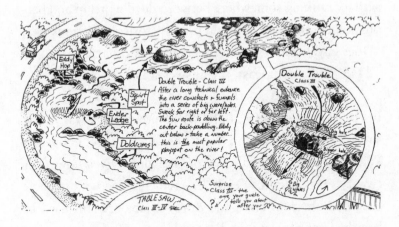

Each one is beautiful, inventive, funny, and practical. In his book *Wild Thoughts from Wild Places*, David Quammen described William's work like this: "[A]n experienced kayaker, a lucid expositor of the hydrodynamics of rivers, and (most notably) a manic cartoonist. Think of him as the R. Crumb of whitewater . . . In his vividly illustrated books he provides vastly more insight into the patterns of flowing water than almost any author I've ever found."

In his maps and books William found the perfect subject for his unique set of skills and passions. They allowed him to merge his love of the outdoors and adventure with a format to express his rough-hewn, self-taught genius, annotated with jokes and asides that encapsulated an entire community and playfully skewered a subculture. "Locals in Appalachia tend to look upon whitewater boating as an activity ranking somewhere between devil worship and heroin addiction." And he could pose rhetorical questions like, "Does kayaking have a hidden metaphysical agenda?"

For William, at least, the answer was yes.

In the span of no time at all, William became a star in the subculture of adrenaline sport aficionados throughout the Southeast and, eventually, across the globe. Even now, over twenty years after his death, he's remembered with the awe accorded an icon. His hand-drawn maps are still used to help boaters navigate the hazardous rapids of rivers across the South: the Chattahoochee, the French Broad, the Haw, Nantahala, New River Gorge . . . To date he has sold over 100,000 of them, all over the world. He most definitely was, no matter what that magazine writer may have thought, a Renaissance man in a neoprene suit, "an intellectual with a chainsaw," as a friend described him.

It's been over thirty years since William published his last book on whitewater, but he has not been forgotten. As a young paddler told me recently: "His instructional books provided unique perspectives on technique, hydrology, and some of the mental parts of the whitewater game. I bought my first Nealy book when I was thirteen, and I still have that same copy, thirty years later. At the same time his cartoons offered a window into the culture of whitewater paddlers. So many times, on a paddling trip," he said, "something would happen that would inspire a Nealy quote, or someone would offer up a bit of Nealy-influenced wisdom, e.g., 'the amount of time you spend staring at a rapid is directly proportional to the amount of time you will spend getting trashed by it.' My senior quote in my high school yearbook was a Nealy quote, much to my mom's lament: 'A mind is a terrible thing to waste, unless you do it right.'"

His good friend Henry Unger, now a professional geologist, described his time with William like this: "It's fun to push it close to the edge," he said. "But we were very calculated about it. Never climbed a mountain without studying first. We pulled out of the river if we didn't know about it, if the water was up too high, know to go left here, better not go right. It was the kind of calculation that keeps you from getting hurt. We never did anything that would get us killed."

William put it differently. In an interview with Kate Geis, who later made a film called *Riversense* in which William is featured, he said that river running, mountain climbing, even mountain biking, were sports that took him "to the edge of death. I think it's very healthy though . . . you have to get near death to really be alive."

Negotiating risk like this is an art, and he did it almost all his life. More than that, he helped others negotiate their own risks: Holly and me, of course; his mother, my mother, his friends; and thousands of people he never even knew, who were and still are guided by his maps. That's what maps are: a way of taking care of people. *Go this way, not that; don't do what I did here, do this instead. It's safer that way.*

Sometimes I would visit Holly and William in the house he built for them, and he would be in his studio, drawing, his ankle literally chained to his drafting table in a shackle as he was finishing a map on deadline, because there were always distractions, there were always so many other things that needed doing. Sometimes a shackle is what it took to keep him on task.

Until the late eighties my life was intertwined with his, with theirs, socially, intellectually, and romantically. My girl-friends were required to like them, and if I noted a whiff of disapproval from either Holly or William, my own affection for these interlopers would abruptly wane. Eventually, I began to date without their approval. On their side, Holly and William seemed to burrow more deeply into their country home with friends I didn't really know. None of us said anything about our shifting dynamic; the world changed too slowly for that, and then too quickly. I started a family, and a micro-business with my first wife, selling my drawings on greeting cards and refrigerator magnets. William drew his maps, and Holly sold them. I wrote novel after unpublished novel, year after year, a one-man production facility for bad prose. In those years that led to the end of the century I saw Holly much more than I ever saw William. When I would go over he would be in the bedroom, reading, or he was napping, or his back was hurting. It used to be Holly who couldn't get out of bed because she was in too much pain; now it was him. Still, Holly presented a joyful front, so I didn't pry and she didn't share.

William was still drawing, though. Years later, after he died, we found several unfinished books: *How to Drive, Living in Trees, Fear Knot!* (a book about tying knots), a memoir about Edgar Hitchcock, and, the best of them all, *Boyz Life*: *Secrets of Male Culture*, which is like the Boy Scout's Handbook for real boys who aren't scared of getting their hands dirty and into just a little bit of trouble. In place of the Boy Scout's "Character, Leadership, Citizenship and Fitness," his table of contents included "Nice Pranks," "Stealth: Ladder Entries," and "Moving in Woods." "How To Do a Wheelie" is there, "How to Trap a Turtle," "How to Throw a Rope." Everything needed to become a boy.

William knew about that. An adventurer, prankster, fisher, and fire starter, always just a step or two away from some bone-breaking, head-cracking, eye-losing moment, close to death sometimes and more alive because of it: William was a boy the way they used to make them, what he would call the *platonic ideal of a boy:* building things and breaking them, fixing them back up again.

But there were two Williams: one was the Man with No Name—the William all of us knew. There was another we didn't know, a man who *wanted* to be named, to be known, the William who lived in his own secret room, the narrow confines of an interior life with space for only one, and a much darker space than I'd ever imagined it would be.

I had tried so hard to be like him, at least like the William I knew, the public William, and now, all grown up, we were the same in so many ways, and different in ways I would not know for years. From that summer's day in 1971 when we met for the first time until the day he died in July 2001, both of us grew and changed, and both tried to find our own reasons to live. But only one of us did.

Part Two

13 Ashes

FOR ABOUT FIVE years, off and on from September 2009 until sometime in 2014, my wife Laura and I kept the ashy remains of four people and a dog in a cabinet in the hallway outside my office at home: my mother, her mother, Holly and William, and their dog, Belle. William died in 2001. His ashes had been delivered to me by a representative of a funeral home in Virginia (William had gone to Clarksville, Virginia, to end his life). The man had driven all the way to Chapel Hill, an hour and a half away, and we met in the parking lot at Whole Foods, and he gave the box to me. I gave the box to Holly, of course—her husband, her whole life in this box—and when she died, I got it back. It was quite a collection in that cabinet, and over the course of the next few years we distributed and dispensed with the ashes as we thought best.

We took my mother to her favorite place, a bay near Destin, Florida. It was marshy, with herons, Spanish moss, and a long dock of weathered wood, pylons festooned with barnacles. So quiet. Laura and I tossed the ashes into the air and watched them settle on the surface of the water before sinking and disappearing in the sand.

Laura's mother Ellen had two send-offs. The first was with her family on a beach in California, and the second was in Vermont where, around a dozen Japanese lanterns, we each sprinkled a pinch of her ashes and whispered our goodbyes and they rose and rose, and the sky was full of her burning light. Then she floated away.

Holly and William were next. Holly died in 2011, fifty-seven years old, a decade after William. She was the only one who'd left clear instructions on what she wanted done with her ashes, and with William's: *I want my ashes mixed together with William's and shaken up and thrown into the air around our house and New Hope Creek. Maybe a smidgen on Daddy's grave.*

It was very simple. I had them both, side by side, ready to be mixed together, shaken up and thrown into the air. All I had to do was fulfill her wishes, everyone would be where they wanted to be, and we could get on with our lives.

But I could not do it.

The ashes remained in my bookcase for a very long time.

The story of Holly's life can be told in two quick brush-strokes: she had been with William, off and on, since she was eleven years old—practically all of her life—and then he killed himself. He was forty-eight years old when he died, and she was fifty-seven. By the time William died, she'd had arthritis for over twenty-five years and over the course of that time had become more and more dependent on him. Because in addition to the arthritis involving vir-tually all of her joints, she also had insulin-dependent dia-betes, chronic sinus infections, total shoulder replacements of both shoulders, right total wrist replacement—the list goes on and on. He was her nurse. He cooked every meal, washed every dish, plugged every leak, fed the dogs and the two pot-bellied pigs, and stayed with her in the hospital, where she spent a lot of her time. She could still drive but only on short trips around town, and she walked unsteadily, with a cane, or drove a scooter. They traveled together in his van, on boating trips, home for Christmas, trips to see friends.

But now he was dead. Worse, he had chosen to die. William, the man to whom she had entrusted everything, her husband and housekeeper, lover, mechanic, driver, partner-in-crime, accomplice, and the other, the most important thing: the man who loved her more than anybody, the same way she loved him. He had left her.

It wasn't surprising, then, that in the weeks and months just after he died, Holly fell into a spiral of grief and madness, manic obsession, whacked-out hyperactivity. Everything she did was an act in some way related to keeping William alive in the world. For her this meant making photocopies of his work—thousands of copies on the most expensive glossy paper she could find.

She gave his art to everybody she could. Laura spent night after night with her, going through files, dumping drawers of stuff onto the living room floor, sorting and re-sorting everything into stacks. Like a balloon whose string was being held in his hand, when William died Holly was released, and now she traveled on every gust of wind, with no guiding mechanism at all. She spent money as if she had a bottomless pot of it, when the truth was just the opposite. But it didn't matter to her. She bought an apartment in Wilmington, North Carolina, right on the harbor. She filled it full of Christmas lights and Doric columns she bought from a local antique store, then went there a few times a month to live that new life. After half a year she lost interest and sold it. "I just wanted someplace where William never was," she told me. But she never found that place; he was everywhere. He haunted her until the last day of her life. (It wasn't until after she died that he started to haunt me.)

She had at least five doctors at any given time. She saw them weekly, sometimes daily, and then there were the operations and the trips to the emergency room, which happened more and more frequently. William had been there for these trips, slept with her in the hospital room, never left her side. He made sure she had everything she would need.

But after William died, I was her plus-one. Most of the time she traveled by ambulance, so I'd meet her at the hospital. On one of our visits, in 2008—I can't remember what we were in there for that time—she was sure she was going to die.

"It just feels like it this time," she said.

"Let's wait and see what a doctor says."

"They don't know anything," she said, and laughed. "I mean, they know *some* things, but not about dying. And they're getting so young. They all look fourteen years old!"

I thought so, too.

"Well, you're not going to die," I told her.

"Just in case," she said, "hand me my purse."

Her purse was a giant cloth bag in which she kept her diabetes supplies and wrist braces and sippy cup of Glenfiddich and her wallet and the lollipops in case her blood sugar was low, the book she was reading and eight or nine other things, among them a notebook and a pen. While we waited on the doctor she wrote out her will, in a frantic, barely legible scrawl.

It was six pages long, a holographic will. Among many other things, this is where she told me what to do with her ashes, how she wanted to mix them with William's ashes, and then take them to the land they used to live on and scatter them around the creek.

She did not die that trip, or the next trip, or the next. It wasn't until 2011, when she went into the hospital to have an abdominal obstruction removed. Her body was just too weak to withstand the procedure.

The last ten years of Holly's life weren't without their joys. She was a wonderful aunt to her nieces and nephews. She traveled a little. She even created a new, alternate family with Raquel and Miguel, a married couple who began by working for her and eventually moved in, along with their two children, and stayed with her until she died.

But nothing was truly good for her again, and that was because of William. As I saw it, he'd done this to her. His decision was the source of all her sorrow. Now they were both dead and their ashes were on a shelf in my bookcase, separate, in limbo, behind a pane of cracked glass.

How long did my ash-duty stay undone? A long time—months. It wasn't as if I was thinking about it all the time, though; it only seems like that now. But since I passed them every time I went into my office I could never completely forget the task ahead of me. I always knew they were there, waiting, as if I could hear their dead fingers tapping at the glass.

In the end, I sent Holly's ashes to my sister Rangeley and she had them buried next to my father's grave on the Eastern Shore in Maryland.

But William? William I kept upstairs, in the cabinet. He was like a character in a myth, one of those stories about a man who's been sentenced by the gods to an afterlife alone in a wooden box, kept from the woman he loves for all eternity.

But the gods weren't doing this: I was.

AFTER HOLLY DIED we went through all her things, every drawer, every box, every treasure. It was the kind of sad day we laughed through, joking, what she would have done were she here. Relief, for her and for us. I don't think it's possible to live deep inside a grief for too long without actually going crazy. I think that was what had happened to Holly.

The last six months of her life she'd been living in the basement of a house she'd just bought. Raquel and Miguel and their two children lived on the main floor.

For someone who was known as being a great collector and creator of very odd and wonderful things (she had encrusted even her headboard and pill boxes herself, with beads, sea glass, and broken teacups), there wasn't a lot that any of us wanted in the end. Barrie took the life-size fiberglass rhinoceros, and Rangeley some photographs and three elephants Holly had adorned with feathers, beads, and decoupage. There was a small painting of a chimpanzee in a nightgown smoking a cigarette I'd always coveted—I remembered being with her and William when they bought it. Laura and I took that and some cement cherubs and a disrobing goddess for our lawn.

But it was as if her life instilled objects with their value; the moment she died, so much of it felt like trash. That coffee mug with the chipped handle she'd bought at the roadside diner that summer; the faux-ostrich feather scarf; the edition of *Catcher in the Rye* she'd read and reread so many times that the pages were falling out, some of them in fact already missing, the tape on its spine yellowed because they'd been taping it up for years, for decades. The lines she loved, they loved, marked and highlighted, the page corners turned back. This was not just a book: it was a relic.

It was in the big green trash bag now, full of everything else that once meant so much to her. No one wanted it anymore.

We went through the day like this, reminiscing and destroying things.

While everyone else was busy going through Holly's art supplies and her miniature scissor collection (she had close to fifty), I explored the small closet beneath the stairwell. In the very back, tucked into the shadows with the spiders and the camel crickets, were two boxes.

I lugged them out into the light. They were full of journals and photo albums. The journals were dated with a black sharpie on their spines: *July 1992–January 1993*; year after year like that. The photo albums were bulging with Polaroids.

"Look," I said.

This was what we said whenever we came across something odd or interesting or valuable or sad or ridiculous. *Look*. They stopped what they were doing. Rangeley came over and removed one of the photo albums. It chronicled a trip out West that Holly and William had taken in the eighties, each photo annotated, along with sight-seeing pamphlets and coasters from bars. Holly and William. So young, so beautiful. We oohed and aahed. Barrie opened the photo album documenting the construction of their home.

I picked up the one that happened to be full of photos of naked people. I looked at a couple of pages, and then closed it, but somehow in that time I was able to see Holly and William. And there were others, too, bodies of their friends, faces I didn't want to see because I was sure I knew them, or had met them, and surely if anything was not my business this was that. I winced as the scenes became more and more Roman (in some of the pictures the women were actually dressed in togas). It wasn't because I objected to their Dionysian past times; I was a big fan of whatever made them happy. But I wasn't a voyeur, an onlooker to some-body else's life. At least, that's not how I wanted to think of myself. It would turn out, of course, that is exactly what I was. Just not so much of the orgies.

One happy thought: if these pictures were any proof, they had a great sex life. In this way as in so many others, they'd used their bodies until they were all used up.

The rest of the boxes were full of the journals, dozens of them.

"What do you think we should do with these?" I said.

There was something about finding them that felt momen-tous, and a little dark, like finding a book of spells. As if by reading them we might accidentally summon William's sad spirit.

"I think we should throw them away," Laura said. She's a social worker. Her job is to think of other people, dead or alive. "They're not ours to look at."

"It does seem . . . invasive," Rangeley said. "And I don't know if I'm really interested in reading someone else's diaries. I don't even like to read my own."

We laughed.

Still, I picked up one journal, thumbed past sketches and drawings and lists and diagrams of dreams and hand-drawn geologic schemata and stopped at a random page. October 27, 1995—six years before he would kill himself. And there it was: "I understand now how people can just reach a point, despite feeling generally good and secure and in love etc. and blow their brains out. It used to build up like snow on a flat roof. Suicide was collapsing under that weight. This is more pure—everything I think I am and love and loves me and etc. is just a bad bad joke—pow!"

I closed it.

"Yeah," I said. "Not sure we want to go there."

"What did it say?"

"Just that . . . he was thinking about killing himself."

"Oh, just *that*?" Rangeley almost laughed.

"Not our business," Barrie said. "Really. It's morbid. We don't have permission."

"He's dead," I said. "How are we going to get permission?"

"Exactly."

So it was unanimous. Just because Holly and William were both dead now, that didn't give us the right to peer so deeply into their private lives. And didn't we know enough already? Enough. This was a purge, after all.

It was a hectic day. So much to deal with. Some friends came over to help and left with a memento or two. I took bag after bag of trash to the truck; Laura and I gathered Holly's art supplies to donate to a school.

I took the journals outside, just to get them out of the way. I should have put them in the truck—it was almost time for a dump run—but I didn't. Without saying anything about it to anybody—even to myself, if that's possible—I put the journals in the trunk of my car. I didn't think about why I was doing this, did not examine too closely what my motivation might be, which is just like me, expert compart-mentalizer that I am. But they were *books*—books by a writer, a famous writer, my brother-in-law. They were one-of-a-kind, handwritten, illustrated, works of art themselves.

But Laura was right: I didn't have permission. I did think of Kafka, of course, and his friend and lawyer, Max Brod. Brod promised Kafka that he would burn Kafka's man-uscripts after he died—but didn't. As much of a betrayal as that was, weren't we happy now, happy that his friend betrayed him? I wasn't comparing William to Kafka when I thought this. I was thinking about the cost-benefit analysis of posthumous treachery.

I took them home without a word to anybody, even Laura. I slipped the journals in the glass-doored cabinet where we kept our rotating collection of ashes. But I didn't look at them again, not for a long, long time.

I think you know where this is going.

Months passed. Holly's house was emptied and sold. The estate, such as it was, was settled. The visions I had of Holly's last seconds alive had faded a little bit, because it was all so fresh. She wasn't taking up an inch of space in the world anymore. Time passed so quickly and before I knew it, months had gone by and thinking of her became more historical than emotional, which was more upsetting: the death of someone you love cuts the deepest wound, but you fear the day it heals.

The difference, though, was that as Holly's death became more distant, and the grief lingered like smoke, a new emotion surfaced, one that was equally, if not more, intense: a searing, almost elemental, hatred of William. It came on so suddenly, as if the spell I had been under all of my life had been lifted. Maybe it was the distillation of hate—or maybe it was just the absence of kindness. The source of it was obvious, born from what he'd done—and left undone. And that of all the terrible diseases Holly had, William had given her the worst of them all: to live the last ten years of her life without him. He'd broken her heart and mind. He'd broken her life.

I reviewed, in a kind of morbid emotional montage, all the operations she'd endured, the late nights in the ER, her last weeks in the ICU—without him. But also what it must have felt like to wake up every morning for thousands of mornings without him in bed beside her, every morning having to remember that the reason he was not here was because he *chose* not to be. That he did not die on a river, or a mountain, or skiing, or riding his bike headlong into a tree, or even falling *out* of a tree. He did it himself. And for thousands of mornings, she had to wake up and wonder if the reason he did it was because of her and the disease that was killing her all on its own.

I despised him for breaking my already broken sister, for abandoning her, my family, me. I wanted to believe in an afterlife I never had been able to believe in, hoping there was a place even now where he might be suffering, and would suffer forever.

But I knew where William was now. He was in the hallway outside of the room where I wrote, in the glass-doored cabinet upstairs.

So I went up there and I got him out.

Then I did a wicked thing.

This was on a night in August 2011. It was late, and even late as it was—past ten, at least—it was still humid, the air was thick and wet and the trees alive with cicadas. North Carolina in mid-August is so hot, and the air at times so still and moist it can feel like you're walking through a swamp.

Laura was downstairs, reading in the family room. The way our house is designed, I can walk from my office into the living room downstairs and out the back door without being seen or heard. This is what I did, through the screened-in porch, using the light cast from the family room—where I could see Laura, on the couch, but she could not see me—and walked to the back of the side yard. It's a place no one ever goes; we've never done anything with it. The soil is dead. Nothing grows there, other than a few weeds now and then; but even they seemed bereft.

It was overcast, no moon or stars. I could see Laura stop reading and turn on the television. Suddenly the yard was colored with that eerie TV blue. Why didn't I have her join me? Why didn't I tell her what I was about to do? Because I thought that if I told Laura what I was doing, she might ask me not to. I couldn't risk that. If I told her, I thought I might change my mind, and I didn't want to change my mind. Which told me that I would most likely regret what I was about to do.

I've never been good at naming feelings, of describing them, or (I fear) even having them. Would it even be possible to separate the feelings out, to see them clearly enough to name them at all? All I know is what I did: I opened the box he was in and began to empty out his ashes. I wandered toward the darker corner of the yard and tossed a handful of him back there as well. Occasionally the ashes would catch a ray of TV light and give them substance, like rain. I knew what I was doing: this was my pitiful revenge on the man I'd spent my life idolizing, who I thought I'd admired more than my father, admired more than anyone I'd ever known. I spread him out—knocking the last bit of him from the bottom of the box with the heel of my hand—until his cigarette-gray ashes were everywhere.

It rained later that night, washing him deeper into the earth as far down as the rain could take him. Had his ashes been seeds, a million Williams would have pushed through the soil and disappeared into the night. But they weren't seeds, they were the opposite of seeds. Like the rest of my family—some who were in the sky now, and some who were in the sea, and one in a grave beside my father—he ended up exactly where I thought he belonged: nowhere. I had liberated him—and thought I had liberated me.

A few centuries ago, people who killed themselves were treated, post mortem, as criminals and vampires. They could be hung, staked through the heart, burned, dragged through the street, thrown into a public garbage heap, put in a barrel and floated down a river—all of this while perfectly dead. The self-murdering hand might be cut off and buried apart from the body, and a stone placed over the dead man's face, to prevent the spirit from rising from the grave. In other words, you got killed twice.

Now I understood why.

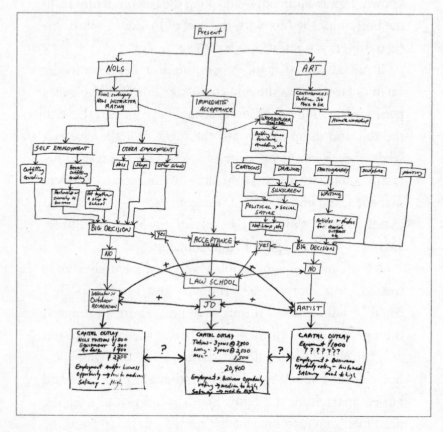

William plans his life.

2013

I SHOULDN'T LOOK at them, I'd always thought that. Or I'd always *told* myself I thought that. I didn't have the right. Reading them would be the worst transgression. It didn't matter that he was dead, the argument went; they were still his. A private journal doesn't suddenly become public just because the person who wrote it is dead, simply because he's not here to object, to stake his claim. Even after the death of a patient, a psychiatrist is still bound by confidentiality. The same logic would seem to apply to journals. Reading them, I had thought, might be the worst thing I could ever do to him.

But after what I did to him that night I realized that, no, reading the journals would not be the worst thing I could do. *I had just done the worst thing I could do.* He was already dead, but—like they did it in the old days—I had killed him again.

I'm not sure now how much time passed. A year, maybe more. Side-eyeing them as I went into my office, I felt like the curious protagonist of a ghost story. *As hard as I tried to rid myself of him, he kept coming back, again and again . . .*

The forgotten archives of a forgotten writer, cloaked in dust, accidentally rediscovered . . .

But I wanted to be done with William. I wanted to erase him from my life. And I was busy. I was teaching fiction at the University of North Carolina in 2011 and writing my fifth novel, *The Kings and Queens of Roam*. I finished it and started another. Laura and I were happy and, after enduring some of the fissures and distractions a long romance seems destined to endure, settled into our lives together with abandon—or what middle-aged abandon looks like: long walks, beach trips, and bingeing *Fleabag* in the light-filled home we had created together, shelves lined with books and miniature treasures, folk art, antique boxes.

So I was putting it off; I was pushing him away. Like William, like Holly, I had a million opportunities to get rid of them. I could have at least boxed them up and put them in the attic. But I didn't.

I pretended to hash it out with Laura, to whom I had eventually revealed their existence.

"Should I look at them?" I wondered aloud.

"Maybe it's not such a great idea," she said.

As if it were like opening an Egyptian tomb when the inscription on it plainly says *not* to, not unless you want to be seriously cursed.

"Yeah. Maybe not. But . . ."

"I can just imagine what's in there."

"I'll look into them. And if it becomes too . . . too awful, I'll stop."

She nodded, but the idea of it seemed to beset her. "Why, though? Why would you want to go back to the worst days of your life, our lives?"

Laura was right, in part. They were the worst days of our lives, but they'd led to some of the best. When William died, Laura and I had been dating for a year and a half. We had just moved in together and had talked about getting married— not anytime soon, really, we never mentioned a date, but it was probably going to happen, at some point, we thought.

But William's suicide consecrated our relationship. It was the first time we had worked together in a tragedy— something we would end up doing a lot in the coming years. Like traveling together and sex, every couple needs to see how the other responds to a tragedy before getting married. It's an important box to check. A few weeks after William died, Laura's father had a heart attack, and she went to Santa Fe to take care of him. She came back on September 7. And then everything changed on 9/11. Laura's brothers lived in New York and had watched the towers fall. Our lives felt transient and valuable in ways we had never had to consider. We were married on September 20, at the court-house just down the road.

Now it was over fifteen years later. Our mothers had died, my sister was dead, William had killed himself. Laura was right. Why would I immerse myself in the beautiful lives that ended in such tragedy?

Her feelings about William were radically different from my own. She didn't meet him until 1999, less than two years before he would kill himself. She hadn't known him, as I had, during his devil-may-care, jumping-off-the-roof days—his bright, brave life.

"All I can think of now is his eyes," she said. "His eyes just seemed very intense. I know this sounds terrible, but he seemed kind of joyless. His dark glasses didn't help. I just hadn't had a whole lot of warm experiences with him." This was true: toward the end of his life he became more withdrawn, quieter. "Holly and William were like a ladder, each side was leaning into each other, and they needed each other so much. He knew that, and that through love and honor and everything that he would take care of her forever. It didn't surprise me entirely that he would die by suicide, except for the fact that Holly was so utterly dependent on him."

"But I didn't have your history with him," she added.

It was just that, my history with him, that compelled me to remove the journals from the bookcase and stack them on my desk. For the first time I counted them: twenty-two. There were a few of Holly's, as well. There were also stacks of loose papers, drawings, maps, mind maps, and one mysterious envelope, separate from the rest. It was sealed with tape, and beneath the tape were strands of my sister's hair.

Together the journals spanned twenty-three years, from 1978 to 2001, the year he died. In 1978 he was twenty-five; in 2001, forty-eight. There were three or four copies of his suicide notes there as well. His driving license, his passport. My heart felt as if it were floating in my chest. Some of the journals were simple spiral-bound notebooks; a couple appeared to be purchased at a Hallmark store. But he favored an orange, hardback five-by-seven-inch field book; the pages were graphed, not lined, and as indicated in the front matter it was "specifically treated for maximum archival service." The graphing allowed him the freedom to write, draw, map, illustrate, design. In the back of each of these field books is a helpful printed appendix that includes a section called USEFUL RELATIONS. *Curvature of Earth's surface = about 0.7 feet in 1 mile. Trigonometric Formulae. The square of any distance, divided by twice the radius, will equal the distance from tangent to curve, very nearly.* These are things William might actually have known, something he carried with him in one of the boxes in his brain.

I opened one at random, and there it was—his handwriting. I so admired his handwriting and had tried to mimic it. I copied him, but not syntactically, or in his style, the way I would later try to copy Carver or Malamud or Cheever: I wanted to write with the literal shapes of the letters he made. Scanning it I could see that every entry was clearly and legibly printed. It was rare to come upon a word I couldn't read. He printed in his journals the same way he printed the text for the cartoons and books he would publish. His letters are rounded and lean right; mine go left or stand straight up, and unless I'm very careful turn into semi-legible smudges, as if I'm writing everything down in a car riding over rough terrain.

That night I organized the journals chronologically, beginning with the first I had: June 4, 1978.

The very first entry:

> I am becoming more & more obsessed with my
> problems—my mind constantly spinning on the axis
> of one or another. Here [in this journal] I will try to
> break down my problem matrix in order to attach it
> on the pages instead of in my mind.

Problem matrix. It reads like an introduction, and it may very well be. It's not impossible that this was his first entry on the day he first began keeping a journal. It's possible that June 4, 1978, was when he realized that there was something wrong with him and he wanted to figure out what it was. He wanted to fix it and he was going to do that through writing about it. But this "problem matrix" became the center of his interior life; through that, his life would evolve and devolve. The journals were not *him*—I kept telling myself that—but operated only as footnotes to his life, or addendums, or qualifiers or fragments of a truth he had never shown to another living soul. *I know who you thought I was,* they told me, *but this is who I really am.*

By the time he died, William seemed to be floating, or swerving, through his own life—not happily or unhappily, necessarily, but like a sailor in the Doldrums, waiting for a good wind. He had Holly, who was devoted to him, a remarkable house, and twenty acres in the country by a river. This is where they'd have what Holly called their "family picnics," summer afternoons on a blanket with their animals—dogs, pigs, rabbits, snakes, whatever they happened to have at the time. It's where he'd take his nephews arrowhead hunting, and where there was a gazebo in the trees that they'd sleep in when they spent the night outdoors. Holly and William had created a truly magical world, the only two people I've ever known who actually lived in their own art. He'd become a legendary figure in the world of adrenaline sports and written ten books. He was strong, capable, and brilliant. Most people would say the same thing his friend Keith Phillips said. "I thought William was living exactly the life that he wanted to live. He had the person he loved, he was doing the things he loved plus he was able to use his art and profit from it."

No one really understood why he did what he did to himself, not even Holly, who had spent most of the days of her life with him. Her own surprise amplified the mystery and intensified the tragedy. How could she have been with this man so long and still be completely astonished by this outcome? How was this possible? Maybe, she said, it was some psychotic break. Maybe it was the medication he was taking. Who knows, she said. We'll probably *never* know.

I've read the journals now, his collected works, and after reading them the question isn't *why* he killed himself; the question is, *Why did it take him so long?*

His journals must be the longest suicide note in the history of the world.

I read them, one by one.

Together they create a remarkable transcription of his life, a compilation of his experiences and troubled existence, and the secrets he kept from us all. They're more and less than that, too. They're his day-to-day life: errands run, pig's cages cleaned, fences mended, driveways plowed after a snowfall, a running pain chart of his aching back. To-do lists. Lots of to-do lists. I didn't have nearly all of his journals—much of an entire decade, the eighties, his golden decade, is missing—but with what I did have, I could reconstruct most of his adult life, day by day. I felt a little like a mad scientist with the DNA of a mastodon captured in a mosquito's larvae, sealed in amber. I could recreate William with his own words with the historical memory drawn from the events transcribed in his journals. Not just the bigger moments—when my cousin died, or when my father died, or when he almost tried to kill himself for the very first time—but what he had for lunch, the books he was reading, the chores he completed and those he didn't, the film he rented to watch that evening—*Romper Stomper*, on April 24, 1994, for instance—along with how many stars he gave it (****). Most of it was nothing, boring really, each detail taken on its own. But when seen as parts of a whole they painted a complete picture of a man, and how essential he was to the functioning of Holly's life, and how hard he tried simply to keep himself busy.

An example:

5 February, Saturday 1993
BP [back pain]—3(2) Full ex
housework—
Holly
3 hr. nap
hotdog dinner
Talked to ma

6 February
BP—2(1) No stretch
Unload van
Anx 3
(feel like I got drunk and/or had affair after H's
breakdown last night)
Fin. clng. van—
Mall, gro, drug sto, vid—pizza lunch—big fade at
3:00 BP—4 1/2 (4)

Errands, napping, cooking, cleaning. Statements of facts, simple events that make up a day. Of the roughly one thousand pages I read, most were like this: shorthand. Lists. One word summaries. In other entries he would mention, in passing, "constant S.I."—suicidal ideation—what he once referred to as "outside voices." But he rarely expanded on it, the siren song of his life, any more than he would the hotdog dinner. The S.I. was like asthma, and his back and knee pain, just another fact of his life. Sometimes he would go into greater detail on seemingly less important subjects, and in the accumulation of detail vividly recreate a moment. In this entry, Holly and William were on their houseboat on Kerr Lake in Virginia:

28 May, Monday 1997
u/a 8—coffee in bed—weather—major front coming through—big hail/tornadoes out Midwest. Wind o/o N. @ 10–15, squalls, lowering skies. Pack up to leave, finish gas decanting, etc. Lv. at 10am—back out into slough—winds pick up—NNE to E on main lake . . . tail wind to Goat I. then NNW wind @ 15-20, 1—1 ½ chop headwind. Wind seems to die as we pass Rosseechi Bluff but picks up big time as we come in—15–25 (halyards whistling). H. gets real peaked after we're tied up. Cold! Hot tea, write in journals, etc. 4 loads sewages (8 buckets) in car . . . Hand clean 2nd 6 gal. tank—3oz. H2o—cart to marina—9.7 gallons and bag of ice. Clean fuel tools, black pan, septic buckets.

Four years later this is where he would spend the last day of his life.

Why did William keep a journal? Why does anybody? The answer seems simple enough: it's a way to keep a register of our days before we forget them. It's something to look back on to remember who we used to be, what we used to do, marking time. And William, like many, used them to provide a space to describe and clarify himself *to* himself. Naming our emotions allows us to understand what we feel and why we feel the way we do—that's the idea, anyway. If we're able to channel what we've learned—our "epiphanies," as William might put it—back into our own understanding of who we are, we can hypothetically live a more enlightened life.

William's style of journal writing was to get everything down, quickly and concisely. He wasn't interested in a narrative of events, or in telling a story (though there are some important exceptions to this); he just wanted to get down the bones of a day, mostly, the facts of what happened, without reflection.

Even so, he was revealed in his journals in ways that stunned me, and that would stun anyone who knew him. It was as if I were reading about another man.

It was easy to imagine how he would feel about all this—me thumbing through the archives of his life—were he alive. Were he alive! What a concept. *Everything* would be different were he alive. An untimely death can shake you to your core, but a suicide will shatter you and you will stay that way for years. And one like William's especially, one that was meticulously planned out over the course of weeks in the midst of us all none the wiser. Were he alive, I would not have been reading his journals at all, but he wasn't alive, and it seemed as if he had left them behind *in order* to be read. One of his final notes on his last of many to-do lists was to "expurgate journals." Not *destroy* them but *expurgate* them: taking out the parts he didn't want anyone else to see. Almost an entire decade was missing. He'd had weeks to dispose of them all as his plan was coming to fruition, and he hadn't. Why?

In 2001, just weeks after he died, Holly had found the journals and read them. She made notes in the margins in a couple of them and had dated one document indicating that she'd read it two weeks after he died. She could have destroyed them as well. But she didn't. How could she? I imagine she read them for the same reason I did: to discover who he was, the nature of that second self that had extinguished both of him.

It's a theme in the journals, the conscious and self-created discrepancy between who he was and who he seemed to be. In an entry in 1995, he spelled it out: "I must not let them see who I really am." But he wrote it in big capital letters, the one and only time he did that in a thousand pages of writing.

I MUST NOT LET THEM SEE WHO I REALLY AM.

And he was successful. He had died a mystery, a master of disguise, unseen.

But he was an artist, at his core, and no artist wants to stay that way forever. We all leave bread crumbs for those who come after us to follow, some of us more than others.

16 His Childhood

HE WAS BORN February 4, 1953, in Homewood, Alabama, an only child. William's father, Willis Nealy, was Superintendent of Parks and Recreation, and is remembered as a quiet man. Every year on Christmas Eve William and his father would toss carrots on the roof of his house, for Santa's reindeer. After William went to bed his father would climb a ladder and replace the carrots with other carrots, ones he had taken a bite or two from. Proof that the reindeer had visited. He died when William was nineteen.

William had severe childhood asthma, which, combined with the pollution generated by Birmingham's steel mills, kept him indoors for a lot of the time. There he would draw and play with his three-legged dog, Prince. Asthma also kept him from participating in sports like football or baseball, so he spent a lot of time in the woods, hunting, fishing, and climbing trees. "I was a Boy Scout," he wrote, "excelling in what used to be called *woodcraft*." He was never into team sports; he was more interested in "individualistic pursuits" like spelunking, canoeing, climbing, and skiing. And drawing. But surely without Scouting and the outdoor skills he learned, he would have become a different sort of person. Scouting and cartooning became the building blocks of his identity.

His mother was a fourth-grade teacher. She sometimes said things that were hard to make sense of. For instance, she didn't like what William was doing with his art and thought he should produce medical illustrations, "because they get to dress up and go to court."

She had written an autobiography of her childhood. Here is an excerpt:

> When it came to pulling teeth, my mother was
> without peer for sheer ingenuity for hair-raising
> techniques. . . . One time she tied a string to my tooth
> and had me lie on my back . . . The other end was then
> tied to my big toe. What was next was Mother with a
> flaming match aimed at my anatomy . . . As Mother
> leaned closer to me with the blazing match, I kicked to
> get away. Sure enough, out came the tooth! It would
> have dropped out in time with far less trauma. But, at
> least, it was an interesting way to extract a tooth.

William was a nerd. He had red hair and light skin and freckles and wore thick glasses, and as a boy he was a punching bag for the neighborhood bullies.

Then, seemingly overnight, he became a man, handsome, desired, courageous, and rash, and that change surprised him. I don't think he was ever able to reconcile these two versions of himself, the strong and the weak, the lonely and the loved. He never really left that boy behind.

Boo Ratley

Rough draft of unfinished cartoon
"Boo Ratley," from the journals

17 Journals II

IN THE HOUSE he built for Holly and himself, William had a
room of his own—an office. He spent hours a day up there.
After doing everything else that needed to be done—the fixing and the feeding, cleaning and constructing—he'd walk
up the winding metal staircase to the attic space where his
drawing table was, and where he kept some of his antique
swords and rifles, an arrowhead display. I can imagine him

taking his last trip to the office for the night, as he made his way through the house locking the doors, turning off the lights, and once there, writing up the day in his journals; he did this, his entries, with a few exceptions, every single day. Then he would walk back down the staircase, get into bed with Holly, and read.

Here his journals were now, taking up two long shelves in a bookcase that he built for me thirty years ago, a library of trouble and woe.

List of ailments, June 1978:

Personal—I Medical / dental
a. worsening of asthma—emotional?
b. Hurt back—lower back strain or climbing related
c. Stomach aches—rel. to overdose of caffeine & vitamins?
d. Dental problem—cavities, broken tooth & no dentist!
e. Psychological dep on drugs

II Personal
a. Holly & her arthritis—I don't know what to do about my rel. @ her
  as she gets worse—> dependence on me grows . . .
b. My socio-economic life—or "what will I do with my life?"

When he wrote this, in 1978, he was twenty-five and I was nineteen. He was, to me, William the Brave, the Capable, the Fearless, the Cool.

But the other William came into focus from the very first pages. I began to see him as if my eyes, after forty years, were finally getting accustomed to the dark.

He struggled. That's mostly what the journals were about—struggle, physical and emotional. *It's been some bad craziness for a while,* he wrote all the way back in 1978. *Last weekend I felt that I was truly headed for the edge.* Page by page, year to year, he was on his hands and knees pulling himself up out of a hole, then tumbling back down, again and again. It's like an action novel starring his psyche. No one got to see the show but him, the circus bigtop of his soul on fire, collapsing around him in slow motion.

He had a plan, though. He knew what he had to do.

He made a list, of course, that very same year:

This is what I must do:
1. Decide what I will be—Adventurer, Cartoonist, Artist, Writer
2. Do whatever is necessary toward that and—
a. write and draw every day on schedule
b. exercise
c. get medical attention
d. assert myself

e. quit being self indulgent—Quit watching T.V.,
   taking drugs, being immobilized, drinking, etc.
f. contribute—write articles, draw, work

Like any good story there are themes and motifs in the journals, not consciously planted by him but arising naturally from the story being told. It's about his desire to do better, to be better, for himself and for others, and the obstacles he faced achieving his goals: his fear, his dependence on drugs and alcohol to escape his depression, and this—a lifelong quandary: *I guess it's some sort of image I'm trying to promote of myself, have been as long as I can remember. I have no one to talk to about my fears and problems because I don't want to drop my facade of "coolness" and macho superiority.*

That couldn't have been it, though, I thought—could it? Was he so invested in this creature he had created—himself—that to destroy it would be, well, suicide? That he was one man for the world and for himself another? That seemed reductionist and simplistic. But as I read this, I thought how lucky I was that, on this count at least, I had escaped the influence of my mentor, the man I'd wanted to become. I harbored few dark secrets; I had no shadow life.

Then I thought about the books I'd written. All of them—including this one—are about people pretending to be someone they aren't. No one in my books was who they said they were. And *their* stories didn't end well either, for the most part. The theme of his life appeared to be the theme of mine, too. Because who am I really? Someone who wanted to turn himself into a writer because he loved the idea of it and didn't know what else to do and so he wrote and wrote and wrote, and it worked. I'm a writer now. But whoever I really am feels just as buried beneath all those pages.

18 Princess Caraboo

ON THE THIRD of April, 1817, a cobbler met a young woman wandering the streets of Gloucester, England. She was wearing a black turban and a black dress, did not seem to know where she was, and couldn't speak a word of English. She was taken to the county magistrate, Samuel Worral, but Worral couldn't understand her either; he had no idea what language she was speaking. He was only able to understand her name—Caraboo. She slept on the floor, washed her teacup by hand between servings, and was drawn to Chinese imagery. But without the ability to explain who she was or where she came from, Worral could do little but take her to Bristol and have her tried for vagrancy, a punishable offense.

From here accounts differ. She is either sent to a hospital or to jail where she is visited day after day by foreigners from the continent, and as far away as China, all of whom try to decipher her language.

But no one could—until a Portuguese sailor came to visit. Even though the language she spoke was *not* Portuguese, he said he could understand her, and he translated her tale thusly: "This woman was Princess Caraboo from the island of Javasu in the Indian Ocean. She had been captured by pirates from her garden and, after a long voyage, she had jumped overboard in the Bristol Channel and swam ashore."

The sailor told this tale and promptly disappeared, never to be seen again.

The Worralls took Caraboo back to their home, and for the next ten weeks she was celebrated for all she seemed to be: exotic royalty. She used a bow and arrow, she fenced, swam naked, danced exotically, and prayed to a god she called *Allah-Talla*. Her portrait was painted and reproduced in local newspapers, and her authenticity was attested to by a Dr. Wilkinson, who went so far as to state that marks on the back of her head were the work of oriental surgeons.

But it was a scam. Someone recognized her from a picture in the paper and outed her. Princess Caraboo was, in fact, a woman named Mary Willcocks, a cobbler's daughter and a servant—a scullery maid—from Witheridge, Devon, where she had entertained children by talking in a language she made up.

Later she went to America, where she was famous—not for being Princess Caraboo—but for having successfully pretended to be Princess Caraboo. She supported herself in America by continuing to pretend, even though everyone knew she was pretending. She was, in other words, being herself pretending to be someone else everyone knew was pretense.

About 175 years later, in 1995, a film called *Princess Caraboo* was released, and when it came out on video Holly and William rented it and watched it at home. This is when William had what he called in his journal the Princess Caraboo Epiphany. He wrote:

> Mary can be the princess and have an adventure and escape the social paradigm, but she's risking it all, to others and to herself. That is the betrayal I'm dealing with—me and the character I've created. It relates to my feelings of imposterdom and alienness and cosmic exposure. Am I one of the two or both?

I understood how William saw himself as a version of Mary/Princess Caraboo, in that they both created personas they tried to sell to the world as "real."

But no matter what William believed, there were differences.

Mary was an imposter. She was never a princess, did not speak a weird foreign language, didn't really sleep on the ground. She'd made all that up; she wasn't real. But *both* of William's selves were real. William hadn't pretended to build houses: he actually had built them. He hadn't pretended to climb mountains, to kayak rivers, to save lives, to sleep in trees, to publish almost a dozen books, to become famous for his gifts and exploits: *he had done these things.* His situation was much more dire than Princess Caraboo's because he knew there were two Williams. He just wasn't sure which was the real one anymore: the hero or the man.

Once unmasked, Princess Caraboo went on to make a good living selling leeches and lived to be seventy-two years old. No one, though, ever unmasked William Nealy. His mask was as much a part of him as the face it covered. He had real skills; he spent his life saving the lives of others. His books are basically survival guides, survival guides for others, advice he never really took to heart himself. *Swim toward the light.* He was always there, all of his selves, but maybe we hadn't tried *that* hard to figure him out. Maybe we'd preferred the mask. He brought talents to the table that no one else in our family had. He built, fixed, and loved in ways we couldn't, or didn't want to, or didn't have to because he was there. And me: seeing him write, publish one book after another, it was so brave—and all the permission I needed to try and do it myself. It's the way we pick out favorite qualities from other people and add them to the human mannequins we are, creating our own unique self in the process. This smile, this jacket, this hairstyle. That death wish? Oh, thanks, but no.

How did I become a writer? Simple: he wrote books, and so I did, too. I had been following him around, in one way or another, since I was twelve, and I had followed him all the way here. But who was I really following: William, or his shadow?

I am only trying to tell you what he said and did, how I see it.

If William was Princess Caraboo, then I am the Portuguese sailor.

$10,000 REWARD

For information leading to the location of missing person, Edgar Hitchcock.

MALE,

5'8" TALL,

120 LBS.,

HAZEL EYES,

SANDY HAIR,

LIGHT COMPLEXION,

WEARS GLASSES

Edgar's car was found in the Eastwood Mall Parking lot Saturday, August 27.

He has been missing since Thursday, August 18.

If you have any information about Edgar, or if you may have seen his car (see photo), please call one of the numbers below.

VEHICLE DESCRIPTION:
1993 Subaru, 4-door sedan, Teal (Blue/Green)

Birmingham Police: Crimestoppers
(205) 254-7777

UAB Police
(205) 934-4434

BPD REPORT NUMBER: 940856208

19. The Murder Book

IT WAS AT the bottom of the box, hidden beneath the journals. Just a sheaf of paper rubber-banded together, pages torn, corners bent, edges grayed with age. A manuscript one hundred pages long, with a picture of Edgar Hitchcock on the cover. In homicide investigations police keep a case file of crime scene photographs, autopsy and forensic reports, transcripts of investigators' notes, and witness interviews—the paper trail of a murder investigation, from the time the murder is first reported through the arrest of a suspect. They call it the Murder Book.

That's what this was, I realized. *The Murder Book of Edgar Hitchcock*. Edgar, the great friend of my entire family, who was charming, funny and lived his life, like William, in a dangerous and edgy duality. In April 1994 he disappeared. He was eventually found months later, in ghastly circumstances, brutally murdered. Soon after his disappearance William and Holly moved back to Birmingham and began to mount their own investigation, making inroads beyond the scope of what the Birmingham police were able to discover.

I only had a general outline of what had happened back then, as I'd lost track of William and Holly. I didn't know the extent of it all—or the nature of it—until I found these notes, all hundred pages of them, detailing their day-to-day inquiry into Edgar's death. William would go out all day, tell Holly what had happened, and she would type up what he told her, often adding reflections of her own. It read like the synopsis of a television show, one I would have liked to watch.

Edgar's scoliosis marked him as being different from almost everybody from the very beginning of his life. His physical weakness defined him in the same way William's asthma defined William. Edgar didn't become a Boy Scout, though: he became a writer. He began writing in elementary school, mostly short stories about tough cops and shady crooks, modeled on the television shows he watched. He would create his own secret agent story, and he would name the characters in his story after his classmates. *I'm going to put you in a story*, he'd tell them, and then get up in front of the class and read it . . . He put the girls in, as the heroines, and some guy would get to be the 007.

In high school he made money writing papers for other students, charging them on a sliding scale, based on the grade they received for it, and in his thirties he wrote humor columns for a local weekly called *Fun & Stuff*. He got the job by approaching the editor and handing him a .38 caliber bullet with the editor's name, BOBBY, written on it in Wite-Out. "This is the bullet with your name on it," Edgar told him. "As long as it's in your possession it can do you no harm." The editor could have the bullet, he said, if Edgar could have the job. He got the job.

And he would write me. *Dear Sir,* his long letters to me began, or *Dear Sirrah, Dear Slur.* Accidental misspellings would be hand corrected. They would end with a *Bemused, Edgar.* Or *In bewilderment,* or *At your leisure.* Sometimes he would adopt a Shakespearean tone for playful banter. *Well well well lad, and what giveth with thou? Prithee, tell me what goes on in that dimlit catacomb mind of thine.*

William had known him, or known of him, since he was a kid, and over the years had developed an almost mystical friendship with him, and he saw the two of them as a part of his own mythos, his own historical-fictional world. In reflecting about their lives together William cast himself as Achilles, and Edgar as Patrocles. Or William was Clint Eastwood and Edgar was John Wayne, or Bob Dylan, or Che. These were the ways William tried to understand who they were to each other, or who he wanted them to be.

"I think because of his poor health and doomed genes," William wrote about Edgar, "he chose crime and intrigue, where I had the physical resources to act on my danger urges on rivers, cliffs, mountains, caves and oceans."

It was only later, much later, that I was able to piece together what a large role Edgar had played in their lives during these years. I was absorbed in my own story, back then, trying to stake my own claim as a writer and, suddenly, as a cartoonist.

A decade before Edgar was killed, I was living in the attic of a house on Oakwood Drive in Chapel Hill, trying to realize my dreams. There was a small refrigerator and a two-burner stove and a sink. There was a couch, a table where I wrote stories on my IBM XT floppy disk computer, and two bookcases William had built for me. I could stand upright only by walking down the middle of the room, beneath the rafters. I had an orange Abyssinian cat named Mister (a gift from Holly) and three bills that would arrive in the mail once a month: a water bill, an electricity bill, and a phone bill. After paying my rent, which was $125, all the money left over—which could amount to almost $200—was mine to spend as I pleased. In the evening I'd put a piece of bread in a cardboard box and tape it up and set it out on the porch, and Mister and I would watch as a raccoon walked all the way up the staircase and tried to open it. It always did. I had girlfriends, but no one steady. I drank beer and smoked cigarettes and wrote, and I remember those days of such utter simplicity as being very happy ones. I wrote in the morning, went to my job at a bookstore (three of them over the years), and then came home and wrote all night. I wrote a lot of novels. One was about five-hundred-pound twin millionaires; another was inspired by a crush I had on a "weathergirl" from my youth. I wrote stories from the point of view of a severed hand and of a talking dog. Not much came of it all. William's career, meanwhile, was ascendant. He had published *Kayaks to Hell, Whitewater Tales of Terror*. In 1990 alone he would publish two books, *The Mountain Bike Way of Knowledge* and *Skiing Tales of Terror*.

When I met Karen, my first wife, I left the attic apartment to live with her. She had two children already, Lillian and Abby. By the time our son Henry was born, in March 1993, I had written two more novels and a collection of stories, none of which were published. I had enjoyed writing them, though. I realized later the sense of joy I had didn't come from making something good, but simply from making *something*, not unlike that rickety table I'd knocked together at the lake. There was no correlation between how I felt about my work and the quality of the work itself. This was both revelatory and disturbing.

I saw Holly and William less and less. When I'd lived alone I'd leaned on them for everything, but now we drifted apart. They weren't that fond of Karen, and Karen did not seem overly fond of them, either. She had two wonderful children she was raising as a single parent, supporting all of them as a waitress. She didn't have insurance—which I saw as evidence of her powerful individualism. Before I moved in with her, she had been living with a woman. She was an outsider, struggling but strong, who (I thought) only needed me to make her life ideal. And she would provide a whole new family for me, too—and one nearly ready-made at that.

I had started drawing cartoons, like William. At first, they were just for Abby and Lillian, drawings I'd place beside their cereal bowls every morning to see if I could make them smile, which was not an easy thing to do at 7 a.m. But the drawings were somewhat charming in their artlessness, and Karen and I eventually started a business selling them, operated entirely from the dining room, to knick-knack stores all over the country. I rarely showed them to William because I thought—I knew—they were so inferior to his. And I didn't have as many opportunities to show him my stuff. We just didn't see each other very much anymore. That sense of a beer-and-smoke-infused Camelot I'd once shared with them was over. Their lives were lived in a different orbit from mine.

I knew where I'd gone, but where did they go? I was only now putting it all together as I combed through all this paper: William was busy solving the murder of his very best friend. How he did it, and didn't do it, is the story that serves as the linchpin of the rest of William's life. And this may go to the heart of how William and I were more different than alike: he was both an artist *and* an actor in his own life. He not only wrote about navigating rivers, climbing mountains, and skiing down them, negotiating treacherous paths on a mountain bike through a forest—he had done it all, too. I had always been more of an onlooker to my own life and to the events that shape me, watching my own story unfold and, like anyone else who might be watching, trying to figure out what happened by writing about it. William was a born detective; I was a born reader of detective novels.

I read the Murder Book, the whole sheaf of papers, William's detailed notes and entries. And I began to feel as if I'd been there along with them; I found myself dramatizing the scenes as if I were there, reconstructing some of the dialogue, but I didn't need to make anything up out of whole cloth. It was just the connective tissue I invented to hold everything together; the bones of the story already existed. Imagine me, an invisible Daniel, watching William be William, a me who was only beginning to see him for who he really was.

EDDIE WAS A PIRATE...

19 Edgar Hitchcock and the Final Frontier

"Selling drugs is the final frontier. It's like the Old West before there was law and order. It's the last really exciting thing a man can do."

—Edgar Hitchcock

JUST FIVE DAYS after Edgar disappeared, William and Holly packed up the van and drove from North Carolina to Birmingham. It was more of a life-support system than a van, carrying clothes and three days' worth of food and Holly's Glenfiddich, fishing supplies, a bed, blankets and pillows, a blaring Nealy-installed sound system, a shelf of books and magazines, a police scanner, a CB radio, walkie-talkies, a box of tools—and a kayak strapped to the top, because you never knew when there might be a river to run. There was also a handgun taped to the underside of the wooden support that William had built for the bed, because once a Boy Scout, always a Boy Scout. *Be prepared.*

The bed was the best part, though. Holly couldn't sit upright for the nine hours it took to get to Birmingham, because of her arthritis. She was still so pretty and cheerful, wrist braces, orthopedic shoes and all, a bright light in a dark room, betraying not a whisper of self-pity. She slept and read, their dog Belle beside her, while William drove, the road rolling into his sunglasses, his face hardened, all business. They were both wearing their nickel necklaces. I can imagine William changing the tape, from the Ramones to Warren Zevon, and turning it up, then turning it up some more until Holly asked him *please* turn it down, just a little. He would turn it down, and then off, and then look at Holly in the rearview mirror. This was his chariot of justice, on the road to find out what happened to Edgar Hitchcock and, perhaps, save him; and if he was too late, he would exact revenge. He was open to whatever high-stakes narrative presented itself.

In all of his work, William had as his subjects three people: Holly, himself, and Edgar. All of his published books were about his own adventures in the natural world, and Holly was always there, his devotion and inspiration, in his books and, centrally, in his journals. And he had tried to write a book about Edgar three or four times over the course of a few years. He was possessed with the idea. They went fishing together, shot guns, camped out, drank, did a lot of drugs—boys being boys. But that didn't explain their almost mystical kinship. They hadn't met until they were in their mid-twenties, and they only lived in the same town at the same time—Birmingham—for a few years, and afterward saw each other infrequently.

So it wasn't a friendship born of longevity, but of something else: they each saw each other *in* the other. It was as if they were made of the same stuff, they just came in different packaging.

On the outside they could not have been more different— William, Tamer of Rivers, über man among men; Edgar, fragile, tiny, who a few hundred years ago might have been a court jester. But they were spiritual and philosophical twins. Both believed that life should be lived on the razor's edge, both had secret lives, and both felt they were destined to die young. Besides Holly there was no one else in the world William would have done anything for, no one else he would have saved if he could. It was only after it was clear that William couldn't save Edgar that the already shaky ground beneath his feet began to slowly, but very, very surely, crumble away. The end of Edgar's life was the beginning of the end of William's.

Arriving in Birmingham, Holly and William met with the old crew at Cosmo's, the pizza joint Edgar had once part owned.

Grendel, Dr. Cheese, Nemo, Red, Captain Midnight, Chili, Cosmo himself—they were all there to brainstorm what might have happened to their missing friend, the old crew with the nicknames earned through their various exploits. Edgar himself had several nicknames: Easy Ed, Squirrel, the Bat, Ocho Rios, Don Bonner, and Fast Eddie.

It was like a wake, or a prewake, a gathering of Edgar's inner circle, all of whom were fearing the worst. Nothing could have brought all these people together in one room other than Edgar. There was so much love, so much shared sadness.

But then there was Stanley Byrd. William didn't know him, had never met him, had never even heard of him. William paused, his hand halfway extended, and a sixth sense kicked in: *What is it about this guy?* Stanley had a broad face, thick dark beard, and a little bit of a mullet. Solid and strong. But he seemed nervous, shaky; he was even blushing. William had a heightened sense of intuition, inasmuch as in his paranoic worldview everyone was a suspect, somewhat untrustworthy, the same way everything is at least a little bit radioactive. But Stanley, whose hand William finally took in his own, was off the charts suspicious. William sensed this in a second. It was a notion that would be lodged into the marrow of his very being and would not be dislodged, not ever, not for as long as he lived.

This man, William thought, had killed Edgar Hitchcock. William was sure of it. He had no evidence, no proof. It was a spark of knowledge conferred as if through the handshake itself. Technically Edgar was just missing now, but in his bones William knew he was dead. And now he knew who did it.

"Good to meet you," Stanley said. "I've always wanted to. Edgar talked about you all the time."

William, of course, couldn't say the same.

And this was when William, instead of simply taking his suspicions to the police—which he did—also decided to conduct his own parallel investigation.

He told Holly his plan later that night: he was going to "befriend" Stanley. Become a kind of double agent, a mole. Go out on searches with him, drink with him. He would keep Stanley close and wait for him to fuck up. "He'll give me something," William said. "Sooner or later, he'll say something he wished he hadn't."

Holly liked this plan. So did the detective working the case, mostly because the police had absolutely nothing else to go on—not a single suspect, not the slightest clue. It was one of William's singular traits, convincing other people to believe in and take part in his obsessions. He was so focused, smart, and confident—or seemed confident, anyway. His greatest power was his ability to project the image of the person he wanted you to think he was. That's why this—pretending to be a friend to the man who might have killed his friend—would be easy for him. He'd had a lifetime of practice.

Lo and behold, the next day Stanley found Edgar's abandoned car in the parking lot at Eastwood Mall. "I decided to think like a criminal," Stanley said. "I thought, how would a criminal hide the car? And I thought, I'd hide the car in a crowded parking lot."

And there it was.

What a coincidence.

Late August 1994. Days passed. No one came out and said it but certainly Edgar was dead, and certainly he had been murdered, and certainly it had something to do with drugs: knowing Edgar and the business he was in, what else could it possibly be? Detectives from the Birmingham Police had combed through Edgar's apartment. Of interest: the tape in his answering machine was missing, and a page from his address book—A–B—had been torn out as well. B for Byrd, among other things. Stanley had told William that he had a key to Edgar's apartment, that he had to have a key because they were "working together." This made sense. Edgar never worked alone; there was always a connection, someone on the other end. But that meant that in the days between Edgar going missing and the missing person report being filed— the entire weekend—Stanley had had access to Edgar's apartment.

Meanwhile, William and Stanley had become insepara- ble. Driving together in the van, conducting a visual search of Edgar's stomping grounds, they shot the shit like old pals.

"I'd like to have twenty minutes with whoever killed Edgar," Stanley said. "If somebody killed him, I mean. To properly interrogate him with a hot knife."

"I hear that," William said.

"I take that back. I'd like to have seven or eight hours with the guy who killed him. You know? I wouldn't shoot him. But I'd cut him up real bad, carve him, make him take amphetamines so he wouldn't fall asleep."

William laughed. "You've been giving this some serious consideration," he said. "The amphetamines are a nice touch."

"CIA/Viet Nam interrogation techniques."

Over the course of the next few weeks William and Stanley would go out on their body hunts, meet up at night to go over their notes, drink, do drugs, and tell stories about Edgar.

Then William would get the group together—Nemo, Captain Midnight, and the rest—and tell them what he'd learned about Stanley. William must have felt he was in his element, becoming the man he had always wanted to be: an operative, a secret agent, a powerful man who alone could solve this crime, who alone would bring justice to his friend, who alone would stop at nothing to get it done.

This was how he would spend most of the next year of his life. I would hear parts of the story later, just bits and pieces. After all of this was long over—in '97 and '98 and '99—William would still be talking about it to people who had never known Edgar.

The year in Birmingham changed him. He assumed the dark, brooding gravity of a man back from the war talking to the civilians, the noncombatants who have no fucking idea what it's like, what he went through. I did admire what he'd tried to do, become the confidant of a murderer, to be a certain kind of person with Stanley, another with Holly, another with me. By the time Laura met him, William would be officially scary—darkly quiet, shaved head, tinted glasses—Conrad's Kurtz. But I didn't see him that way. I'd known him for too long. I thought he was awesome.

The flawed ideas we have of the people we love the most are the hardest ones to surrender.

William's double life consumed him. Eventually he was one of the only friends Stanley had; William had made certain of that. The more he was able to convince the rest of Edgar's friends that Stanley was the murderer, the more isolated William was, and the stronger his hold on Stanley became.

He went through Stanley's trash, piece by piece, looking for evidence; they even called in a fortune teller. She tried to channel information from one of Edgar's Hawaiian shirts. She had a vision. "He was killed near a T-shaped pond," she said. "In the middle of maybe thirty acres or so. He was on his knees . . . and they shot him. The body is lying near the water. I also see some pine trees nearby."

Pine trees. That narrowed the search area down to . . . the entire Southeast.

None of them wanted to believe her—Edgar on his knees with a gun to his head, his body collapsed in the pine straw, lazily covered by the few leaves they could find—not even bothering to dig a grave.

Still. Psychics were experts at making up stories, and this one seemed unusually cruel. This is what William was thinking. She'd gone too far, spruced her story up with too many unnecessary imaginary details. Because the tale she told of what she thought might have happened to Edgar could not have been more horrifying. Something terrible had happened, but nothing this terrible.

Oh, how wrong they were.

Like my father would say later: *You lay down with dogs and you get up with fleas.*

What happened in Birmingham, what happened after, what it led to, how it all fell out, is one of the saddest stories I know. I don't know if I can do it justice. I try to keep my authorial distance, but there is a difference in writing about the life and death of someone you knew and loved and writing about a character who exists solely between the covers of a book, no matter how much time has passed between the event and the recording of it. If this were a novel, I would delight in the darkness I had created for my characters, this apparently hopeless realm of hell into which I had them descend, knowing that I had it within my power to save them. But I'm powerless here. I can only watch as the story I already know unwinds to its ending.

Days and nights they spent together, William hoping for that moment in which Stanley would betray himself, the guilt too much for him to bear, the moment he would admit to everything. But it never happened. All William managed to learn was that Stanley had been one of Edgar's closest friends. That Stanley housesat for him, that Edgar took care of Stanley's dogs, that he had reason to think Edgar and Stanley had most likely been working together over the course of the last few months, buying and distributing coke and dope. That they were a team, the kind of team Edgar and William might have been, had William not left Birmingham for North Carolina. Who knows. One night William wrote how he and Stanley had gone out drinking and then drove to Stanley's place where they did coke until 2 a.m. Stanley got out one of his guns to show William, a Sig. 226, a handgun favored by police and Navy Seals. They both loved guns so much. "We fondled it," William wrote, "and sorta laughed about our sicko hobbies."

William called this *deep cover*. But in reading about his fixation on Stanley, the accidental admiration he had for him, it was clear Stanley had become William's friend, too.

Months passed with no news, no progress, just the same old mystery. Stanley sold his house and moved to Colorado and if this wasn't proof he did it, William didn't know what was. But you can't charge someone for murder just because they move away. The police lost interest in the mysterious disappearance of a drug dealer.

And then Edgar's body was found, and everything changed.

• • •

From the Murder Book:

> On Thursday, January 12, 1995, a construction worker
> rehabilitating an abandoned apartment complex near
> Eastwood Mall finds a human foot in a breezeway and
> calls the police. The police find Edgar's body, what's left
> of it, wrapped in a piece of carpet, stuffed in a storage
> closet on the deck of an apartment unit.

This is where Edgar's body had been, presumably, for
nearly six months. Six months wrapped in a piece of carpet in a storage closet, with only a little plywood between
his body and the weather. That's where he was in August,
the hottest month of the year, and into September, October,
November, and December. Edgar's body was blackened,
entirely desiccated—skeletonized. There was no face, no
skin, but his hair, that furry afro, was still there. Though
they would use dental records to identify him, it wasn't
really necessary: you could see the Harrington implant, his
spinal rod made of stainless steel, clear as day.

What was abundantly clear was that someone had gone
to great effort to make Edgar dead. He was shot five times:
in his head, in his chest, and in his arm. Three ribs were
broken, and so was his clavicle. His skull was fractured. His
mandible was fractured. His ulna was fractured. Some bullets were still in him, while others had zipped right through.
But the first wound was probably the one in the palm of his
hand, the hand he raised in self-defense, as if it might stop
the bullet he knew must have his name on it.

All this done to a man who could have been broken in half in an overzealous hug.

The funeral, from what I heard, was one of the best there ever was.

"There are so many beautiful women in black," Holly wrote in the Murder Book. "Dozens and dozens of beautiful women, little girls and old women, elegant women. Oh, Edgar would have loved to see this."

Even Stanley returned from faraway Colorado to pay his respects.

William read a poem, from *archy and mehitabel* by Don Marquis, called "the lesson of the moth." In it, a moth is explaining why his kind fly into light bulbs:

> we get bored with the routine
> and crave beauty
> and excitement
> fire is beautiful
> and we know that if we get
> too close it will kill us
> but what does that matter
> it is better to be happy
> for a moment
> and be burned up with beauty
> than to live a long time
> and be bored all the while
>
> . . .

it is better to be a part of beauty
for one instant and then cease to
exist than to exist forever
and never be a part of beauty

Edgar's casket was a wooden box with a heart-shaped knot in it. After almost everyone had left, William went back to his van and got a "grave goods" package he made for Edgar. In it was a crushed red fez, a saber, a Savannah point knife and arrowheads that he'd made, assorted pictures, a medicine bundle, a tooth, herbals, a deck of cards with the Queen of Hearts showing, hand-tied fishing lures, and from Holly, an Indian blanket wrap with hawk feathers and beads.

The Monday after the funeral, William and Stanley met for lunch. Both seemed beaten down with grief. Stanley told him how hard it was for him to be back, when so many thought that he was involved in Edgar's death, either that he'd killed him, or had him killed, or was there when it happened.

William and Stanley reminisced. They talked about guns, how Stanley and Edgar had gone shooting together sometimes, how lonely he was in Colorado, how hard it was to meet girls. "I'm depressed," he confided to William. "I was at Cosmo's this afternoon and no one would sit with me. People actually got up and moved away."

But not William. William was sitting right there with him.

Outside, beyond the big picture window that looked out onto the street, Southside's indigent shuffled past. Then Stanley said the oddest thing. "How about us going to that apartment complex, the one where they found Edgar."

"What?"

Stanley said it again and it still didn't make sense.

"Let's go see where it happened."

"But Stanley," William said. "We don't know where it happened."

Everyone knew about Mountain View, the enormous abandoned complex where Edgar was found. But no one, other than the police, knew exactly where, in which apartment.

"You don't know, do you, Stanley?"

Stanley shook his head. "No idea," he said. "But nothing ventured, right?"

And William probably thought: *This is something Eddie and I might do.*

So William and Stanley went on an adventure. As a crime-fighting duo, it would be their last.

The winter sky was a blanket of gray, the sun dull behind it, no warmer than the moon. William picked Stanley up at a friend's house. Stanley couldn't stop talking, but in a weird, anxious way.

"I've been thinking," Stanley said. "I ran into a guy I hadn't seen in ten years or more, and he knows this guy who just got out of prison. Used to deal around here, was a part of this . . . homo-cocaine ring."

"A what?"

"A homo-cocaine ring," he said. "Anyway, a real professional. I'm just saying that if he was involved in this we better be careful, because they are *real* professionals."

"I've never heard of a homo-cocaine ring," William said.

"Real professionals," Stanley said.

Stanley stared out the window.

William turned into Mountain View Apartments. He'd thought about it a little bit, the best way to go about the search. His plan was to drive to the top of the road, far away from construction workers busily remodeling the complex below, and then work their way down. It made sense: if your plan was to kill someone and hide the body, better do it as far away from everybody else as possible. But about halfway up the road Stanley said, "Turn here. This looks good."

Why did it look good? There was nothing that distinguished this turn from any other. But William did as Stanley said. He drove another hundred yards or so, to a cluster of four apartment buildings at the end of the road. There were five identical clusters above and below it. Jesus. What a day they had before them. An impossible day. But as William slowed down to park he saw a garbage can in front of him, one he couldn't see from the main road. The tail end of bright yellow tape was hanging over the edge.

Police tape. Crime scene.

"Well look at that," Stanley said. "We're getting warm."

"It'll still take us a week to go through all these buildings, Stanley," William said.

"Unless we get lucky." Lucky, he said. "We might as well try."

Stanley got out of the van first and walked toward one of the buildings.

"Let's try this one," he said.

William felt like he was being dragged into somebody else's dream, the way Stanley was in control now, *turn here, go here, let's do this.*

They tried that building.

So still and empty inside. The unpainted walls, floors coated in drywall dust. Some of the doors didn't even have knobs on them. William played with a wall switch: no lights.

They peered into the first apartment they came to. Carpeted, even a sconce on one wall. But all the outlets were empty, waiting for switch boxes. William could hear Stanley breathing not far from his right shoulder. As William was set to explore the interior Stanley said, "This isn't it."

"It's not?"

"It's too dirty," he said. "Shit everywhere. Evidence guys would have really cleaned it out."

On to the next apartment, #2 of eight hundred or more. But this time Stanley didn't even bother to follow him in. This one, too, was full of sawdust and orphaned two-by-fours, a styrofoam cup, the dead end of a cigarette.

Same for #3.

Then, in the breezeway leading to the fourth apartment, they saw somebody. A site boss. A short, heavy, jowly man wearing an orange vest and a yellow hardhat. William introduced them both, by name, and explained that their friend Edgar was murdered here. "We want to see where it happened," he said. "The detective on the case said it's okay," William said, and the lie seemed to work.

"If my boss was here he'd have you arrested," the man said. "But he's not. This is it here."

"Here?" William said.

The site boss pointed. It was the apartment they were just about to enter.

"Bingo," Stanley said.

"Go on," the site boss said. "I'll let you look around for a minute or two."

William and Stanley walked to the center of the room and stopped. The room was immaculate, cleaned, even dusted. You could imagine a couch here, with a coffee table, and television on a stand against a wall.

But some of the carpet was missing, a swath of it about the size of a small person.

"That's what they used to roll the body up in," the site boss said. "That carpet."

William's mind was humming with static, a radio between stations. He couldn't get past the simple thought, the bleakest thought, that he was here in the last place Edgar was alive, and that he was in it with the person who may have been here with him.

He walked out on the deck, alone. There was the storage closet. It was small, the door about three-quarters the size of a regular one. Stanley hung back, inside with the site boss, yammering in his speedy rush. "Edgar was the best," Stanley was saying. "So many people loved him. We were really close. Tight."

William opened the door to the closet and looked inside. It had been vacuumed, totally spotless. But he could see the stain on the concrete floor where Edgar's body had seeped, the smell still suffocating after all these months.

William felt a bile climbing up his throat. What was Edgar doing here in this godforsaken place? What brought him here, alone? He was too smart for that—too paranoid. He would never have gone to a remote apartment complex by himself, without backup, unless it was to see someone he really trusted, or if he had been sent there by someone he really trusted. Like Stanley.

He closed the closet door and walked back into the apartment, where Stanley was still making conversation.

"The police found a shell casing in here," the construction worker said.

"Really?" William said, still dazed, still feeling like he was falling off a mountain.

"A nine-millimeter semi-automatic?" Stanley asked

No one had told anybody what kind of gun was used to kill Edgar.

Outside the sun was breaking through a cloud, and the light in the room changed. William could see where the spattered blood had almost been washed from the walls. It was on the floorboards, too, not far from where the carpet used to be.

Stanley and William walked back to the van. "I shouldn't have said that about the gun being a nine-millimeter in front of the construction guy, should I? It sounded suspicious. Like I know. Like when I found the car. It was just a guess."

William told him not worry about it. Started the van, drove out of Mountain View. But the fact of it hung like smoke between them.

William thought Stanley knew too many things. He had been the one to "find" Edgar's car, but as unlikely as it seemed, that could be explained away. Not this, though. Coming here seemed as good as a confession. *Why would he have brought me here?* William wrote in the Murder Book. He must have known this would tip the scales. Was it guilt? Did Stanley wanted to impress him?

Or maybe Stanley was just that dumb.

Stanley and William talked on the phone the next day. Holly was still asleep, and my mother was out walking her dog before the rain that was supposed to happen later in the day.

"I'm still worried about that nine-millimeter semi-automatic weapon statement," Stanley said.

"Yeah, well, I wouldn't worry."

"They've brought me in twice already." He didn't ask how many times they'd brought William in, because he probably knew: none. "I feel like . . . I just don't feel good about it."

William tried to give Stanley the benefit of the doubt—not because he wanted to, or because he deserved it, but because William wanted to be certain. He factored in the possibility that Stanley could have guessed the caliber of bullet used. The chances that it was a 9mm seemed pretty good.

But then William calculated the odds of Stanley guessing the apartment where Edgar had been killed. There were 58 buildings, 3 levels in each building = 1/174.

William believed there was only one way he could have known this. Only one.

"You know," Stanley said, "I don't like people, as a rule. I like animals more. But if I ever found out you weren't my friend, I would lose all faith in humanity."

"Don't worry about that," William said.

And then, hanging up, he called the detective and told him what happened with Stanley. The next morning Stanley was arrested and charged with capital murder. The lede in the *Birmingham News* highlighted the irony of it all: "A man who returned from his new home in Colorado to attend the funeral of a slain friend has been charged with capital murder in the case."

All the evidence was circumstantial, but most evidence in criminal cases is circumstantial. They still felt they had a good case.

A grand jury agreed. This meant it would go to trial, and William believed that Stanley would most likely be convicted. And in Alabama at the time, murder was a capital crime; were he to be found guilty, he would die in the electric chair.

William was victorious, a hero like Odysseus, or Achilles, or Clint Eastwood.

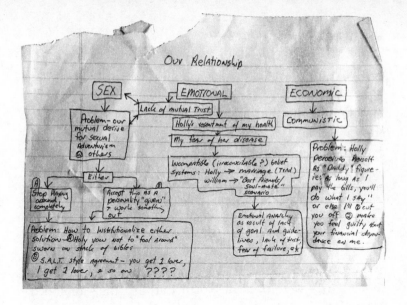

20 Coming Home

THEY WENT HOME now, home to the house William had built for them deep in the Hillsborough woods. It felt, and was intended to be, a place apart from whatever existed outside its fences. Surrounded by twenty wooded acres and New Hope Creek, it might as well have been its own city-state. Driving down Elvis Presley Blvd. and through the gate, the top of which was lined with the heads of dolls turned inside out (William's take on the ancient practice of mounting the heads of your defeated enemies on a pole), it felt—as you might imagine—that you were entering another world. They were greeted by Sherman and Harold, the two pot-bellied pigs they adored, lumbering out of the small pink pig house with Ionic columns that William had built for them, past the life-size fiberglass rhinoceros to the right of the covered walkway leading to the house, and in the grass, dozens of elves and dwarves and painted rocks and concrete angels.

While Holly and William were searching for Edgar, and William's spy-routine absorbed him, it was easy to be distracted from their own lives. But when that drama faded into the background, the challenges they faced as a couple—the physically faltering Holly and the emotionally faltering William—came into an unambiguous focus. Almost as soon as they were back in North Carolina they imploded. They began to fight over everything.

Their issues were real, but they were also variations on ones decades old. To get along in his life William needed something to direct his vision outward, away from himself; otherwise, he was drawn inescapably inward, and there was almost nothing good for him to see in there. That's why he'd dedicated his life to death sports; that's why he'd become a paramedic, an EMT, why he was determined to save the people closest to him and even those who weren't, those strangers on the river, on a pair of skis, on a bike. And it was why he became so obsessed with Edgar's case and why his obsession eventually became less about Edgar than it did about the hunt.

In other words, just when they might've felt some resolution—Stanley in jail and charged with capital murder—it was the opposite. William descended into his darkest place, and on February 3, the day before his thirty-second birthday, he tried to kill himself, sort of, for the very first time.

He wrote about it.

February 3rd, 1995. "Marriage counseling. Very sad, disappointing, etc. Big fight after . . ."

Then: "More fighting—re: my obsession/insanity over Eddie case . . . [Shotgun] to head, like scene in *Blazing Saddles.* H and I wrestle with the gun.

"My whole life," he goes on to write, "has been a struggle against the world to preserve my 'being' and it's put me in dire conflict with the people I love and depend on the most . . . Most of my suicidal ideation has to do with this action-less helplessness I feel in social and intimate situations. I MUST NOT LET THEM SEE WHO I REALLY AM! I like the guy—one of the coolest guys in the world—I don't know if they can handle the real me." I could feel his desperation by drawing my finger across the indentation in the paper itself.

But the truth was, it wasn't us who wouldn't have been able to handle the real William Nealy. The only person who wouldn't have been able to handle the real William Nealy was the real William Nealy himself. Reading this made me want to reach out to him backward through time and hold him.

In an interview with the *Independent,* a local weekly paper, in 2003, Holly described the attempted suicide like this: "He went in the dining room and got a rifle and put it in his mouth. And I, of course, he was so strong, if he had wanted, I could not have literally reversed his physical movement had he been intent on it . . . he could pick me up with one hand."

The day-to-day slog of even the darkest existence is made bearable when at the end of it all there might be a payoff for simply enduring. For William that would've been Stanley's trial. The man who he thought killed his buddy would be sent to prison for life, or maybe even killed in the electric chair.

The trial was set for October 1995—not too long to wait. But then it was reset to March 1996. Delays, especially for murder trials, are very common.

Then the original prosecutor left for private practice, and the trial moved to May while the new prosecutor was brought up to speed. Holly and William drove back to Birmingham and met with him and went over their notes in the Murder Book.

And then another prosecutor was assigned to the case, so the trial was reset again to July, and was postponed again until October 1996, exactly a year from the original trial date, and then to January 1997, and finally March again, when a fourth prosecutor was brought in to take the place of the third.

So much time passed. The evidence was deemed circumstantial. Prosecutors are averse to taking cases to a trial they might lose, and so in July, the charges against Stanley Byrd were finally dropped, due to insufficient evidence.

There would be no trial.

The news came in a phone call from Edgar's sister Amy, and on that day William wrote a single-word journal entry: *Homicidal.*

It wasn't the first time he felt this way about Stanley. From 1994 to 2001—to the very last day of his life, in fact—William fantasized about killing Stanley Byrd. Stanley possessed William like the ghost of a still living man, and there was nothing William wanted more than for Stanley to die and possess him like a proper ghost.

But William never could have killed Stanley: William, for all his bluster and seeming darkness, could never really hurt anyone. He was the kindest, most gentle man you would ever want to meet, and Edgar was the same. Maybe Stanley is, too; his friends say he is. I've never met him, so I can't say myself. Killing Stanley wouldn't have helped William anyway. In a way it was better for William that Stanley lived, because Stanley had become the repository for his rage. To William, Stanley stopped being *Stanley*, I think—stopped being a real live human being. He became a symbol of evil, the essence of all that was wrong with the world, the darkness no light could brighten. He was an imaginary monster, and even though he lived in William's mind and William's mind alone, William could never have killed him. Once it was clear that Stanley would not pay for what William believed were his sins, William was in an impossible place of torture. He felt there was no justice in the world. Despite all the care and love he brought to saving Holly, he was no match for the illness that was killing her. The good die young and the guilty go free. His best friend was dead. William had failed him, and now he wanted out himself. He'd actually been looking for an honest exit for a while. Still, it took him a few more years of puzzling through it all to realize that he didn't *have* to kill Stanley. It wasn't required. He released himself from that dreadful duty.

Only one of them had to die.

21 Hindsight

TWENTY-FIVE YEARS LATER, I went back to Birmingham to reopen all the old wounds. Edgar was dead, William was dead, Holly was dead, too, and I believed—though their deaths could not have been more different—that their deaths were connected by an unsustainable loss, each leading to the other like falling dominoes. I wanted to solve the case for all of them. Would there be any better way to consecrate their memories, to end this story the way they would have wanted? Not to become a hero myself, but to acknowledge William's heroism, to show him that he did teach me a thing or two about love, friendship, and taking care of those you love the most?

In Southside there is a place called Hitchcock Plaza, but the plaque with his name and face on it kept getting stolen, so it was hard to find. I spoke to everyone who would talk to me, all the witnesses: Grendel, Dr. Cheese, Nemo, Red, Captain Midnight, Cosmo. Everyone but Chili, as I didn't know who Chili was. No one had any insight that they hadn't had a quarter of a century before, probably even less so given that so much time had passed. I went to the apartment complex where Edgar's body was found. I spoke to lawyers, an ex-senator, Edgar's brother and sister, friends with an axe to grind, friends without an axe to grind, a couple who wanted to set the record straight and a couple who didn't. Everywhere, there was such great love for Edgar.

More than anyone, though, I wanted to talk to Stanley Byrd. I hired a P.I. to track him down. He was living in the Southwest, where he moved after the murder. I sent him five letters and he didn't respond to one of them. I tried to explain to him that I didn't think he was a murderer; I just wanted to find out what really happened, that so many people would like to know. This didn't sell him on the idea. Finally I was able to connect with one of his old girlfriends who was still in touch with him. I asked her to ask him if he would talk to me, and she did, and he told her no way. "He is flat-out not interested," she said.

I understood. There's no statute of limitations on murder, and in Birmingham there were people who still thought Stanley did it. But no one had any *reason* to believe he did, other than William had told them that's what *he* thought. And he told a lot of people that's what he thought.

Then I spoke to one of the prosecutors. Though all of this happened almost a quarter of a century ago, and she had been retired for ten years, she remembered the case well. I asked her why the case hadn't gone to trial.

"There was no eye witness, no fingerprints," she said. "A jury has to decide that *all* of the circumstances point to the guy and *no* other potential hypothesis could hold up. If it's possible that someone else did it, you're out.

"Statements fell apart at pretrial. Things didn't add up. If we had gone to trial, at the conclusion of the case the judge would grant a dismissal. If it was dismissed, we would never be able to charge again. We wanted to wait and see if something else came forward."

Nothing did.

And just like that, it was over.

I thought back to all the time and energy and sacrifices Holly and William made to get Stanley Byrd to pay for what they thought he did. How they left their home behind to return to Birmingham to see justice done. For what?

Then she told me something that changed my perception of everything.

We were talking about William, and what he did to try and solve the murder, how much it meant to him. She said she could tell that he was obsessed.

"This is one of those occasions," she said, "that close friends went out on their own, looking for evidence and talking to people. With so many people sharing information, it was hard to find information that wasn't tainted. No witnesses who could say *I specifically saw this*. They only *heard* someone say it—William—and they never could find the source.

"Stanley was a good suspect. *But once you get in mind that he did it, everything you see is in the context of him having done it.* You see it through those glasses. Wrapped up in Edgar, and focused on the hunt, absorbed by it—that created passion, and undermined the witnesses. William would pull together all these people comparing stories with one another. He may not have been responsible, because they might not have been able to convict Stanley anyway. But it made it much more difficult. All the talking undermined it."

She was suggesting that it was possible that Stanley Byrd might have been convicted had William and Holly never returned to Birmingham at all. I didn't know whether this was true or not, and neither did she.

"Did you ever tell anybody?" I asked her. "I mean, could William have known?"

"No," she said. "There was no sense in telling him. What's done is done."

A good thing that she didn't. I think he would have killed himself even sooner if she had.

But he tried so hard to live.

In July 1997, just after the charges were dropped and Stanley became a free man, William made another one of his lists, the ultimate Pro/Con list: should he live or die?

Pro: I have a woman I love, a beautiful home and land, sufficient income, tons of paraphernalia, a houseboat, a profession, pursuits I love: primitive tech, artifact collecting, archery, bicycling, shooting, woodsman-ship, geology, woodwork, flint nap, 10 books, limited fame, good writing ability, phys. healthy mother with good insurance and good estate.

<u>Con</u>: *Alcoholism, drug dependence, chronic shyness, poor concentration, low self-esteem, insomnia (chronic), passive aggressive personality, unipolar depression, S.I., <u>paranoia</u> neurosis, D.D.D. x4, asthma, cig. addition, sick pets, fogged thermopane, termites.*

The scales were weighted from the beginning. Still, he would live for another four years with the woman he loved in their beautiful home, fogged thermopane and termites notwithstanding.

22 The Immortality Project

THE EARLIEST ENTRY I have in William's journals is from July 1978. He was twenty-six years old. He was working in a trail shop at the time, and just starting to draw his maps. In this entry he writes about many things, but for me the most interesting section deals with the concept of an "immortality project."

It began with an argument he had with Holly. Apparently, she had asked him if he'd been depressed lately, and she told her he'd been sad for a very long time. He told Holly that "my problem, at the root of it all, was that I lacked a CAUSA SUI project—an immortality project—a consuming task."

He was reading *The Denial of Death* at the time, by Ernest Becker, and this is one of the big ideas in the book. "An Immortality Project is one in which we create or become part of something that we feel will outlast our time on earth. It's how we hope to become heroic, and part of something eternal—the belief that our lives have meaning, purpose, and significance." Becker also argues that "the basic motivation for human behavior is our biological need to control our basic anxiety, to deny the terror of death." This is why we distract ourselves with greater goals, like saving lives, solving crimes, or even writing a book.

Reading William's journals, I came to realize that this idea was true for him, then and throughout the rest of his life. Maybe the truest thing. He needed to have a project—small projects like replacing a rotten piece of wood on the deck, and larger ones, like my sister. Holly was his first immortality project. He thought that through his sacrifice and devotion to her maybe he could save her. That she could be his consuming task. That was why he'd stayed with her, way back when. I knew that he'd loved her more deeply than anybody else in his life, but if she had never gotten sick I believe he might have left her, that he'd stayed not despite but *because* of her illness. It turned out that he couldn't protect her against a ravaging autoimmune disease, which tore at and disassembled her and was, in his words, "like watching your lover being raped and mutilated every day for 20 years." So, no heroism for him there, even though to my mind, staying with her in the first place, and making her life possible in the second, was the heroic act.

Then there was Edgar. When William learned that he was missing, his first hope was to find him, somehow, alive. It was unlikely, of course, but this is the sort of thing heroes do: it's what distinguishes heroes from the rest of us. Look at his books: chapters are spent on rescue and self-rescue. *Don't give up! Swim towards the light!* And once Edgar was found dead, there was always a backup plan: justice, which was a kind of revenge. That was a good project, and this one almost worked. William did his part, he found who he thought was the guilty party, but felt that the justice system failed him. And as much as some journal entries suggested he wanted to, he could not take matters into his own hands and deliver a different kind of justice. He couldn't kill Stanley. It just wasn't in him. All he could do is fantasize about it, creating more intricate and creative ways to kill him as the years went by.

It started to feel to me like Edgar was William's last chance. Had he solved his murder, he *might* have saved himself. Edgar could have been his redemption, a redemption he didn't really need—he had given so much of himself already—but only imagined he did. Avenging the death of his best friend (what Achilles had done for Patrocles) would have allowed him to bring a balance back into the world, into his world at least. It would be a story we'd be telling for a long, long time, a story about a hero who finally got his Elysian Field upgrade. He may have hoped for another opportunity, but over the next four years one did not present itself. Instead, he developed four herniated discs from a bike accident, and then he couldn't paddle. He could barely sit long enough to draw. To himself, he was just the shell of the man he'd built for himself to live in, a would-be hero who never had a real chance to be heroic, a man who nobody really knew.

But there was something else that Ernest Becker wrote that I kept coming back to. I didn't know if William ever read it, though; it was in another book, *The Birth and Death of Meaning.*

"By the time we grow up," Becker writes, "we become masters at dissimulation, at cultivating a self that the world cannot probe. But we pay a price. After years of turning people away, of protecting our inner self, of cultivating it by living in a different world, of furnishing this world with our fantasies and dreams—lo and behold we find that we are hopelessly separated from everyone else. We have become victims of our own art."

We couldn't save him for the same reason he couldn't save himself: no one, not Holly, not me, maybe not even William, knew exactly who he was. Odysseus, Achilles, Princess Caraboo, Clint Eastwood. The Coolest Guy on the Planet. All, some, or none of the above.

23 The Envelope

IT WAS IN a folder where I kept documents that didn't fit anywhere else. The journals had an entire shelf in my bookcase, but there was so much more: two miniature journals that were the size of index cards in which he wrote in letters almost too tiny to read. There was his driver's license and passport and a picture of Elvis Presley on a plastic change tray, loose photos, random notes and loose-leaf papers, a few drawings—and the envelope. On the front Holly had written "H [Holly] read 9/02/01." And a description of its contents: "William's intense self-hatred."

And on the back, of course, that tape across the seal and the hair beneath it.

Holly had dated it, fifteen days after William had killed himself. Two weeks. I'm assuming she had just found the envelope that day. She was drawn to it immediately, as I was, because this was different from the rest of the material, separate, specific. I couldn't open it, but she did. She opened the envelope, read its contents, read it again, I imagine, and again if she could stand it. She sealed it, and then she removed five long brown hairs from her head and taped them to the seal.

Why did she tape her hair to the seal? Was it a safeguard, that if anyone were to open it, she would know? Or was it just to say that what was in this envelope was so precious, so *dangerous*, that she had to mark it with a part of her body? All I know is that the hair across the seal distinguished it mightily from anything else I'd ever held in my hands.

She did what she did. Then she put the envelope away, and for the next seventeen years it was never opened again. She didn't date anything else; none of the journals, which she no doubt read as well, had her mark anywhere on them. She dated this because—I don't know why. Maybe she just wanted to mark the day when she finally learned everything she needed to know about him.

Now it was mine. It wasn't mine, really, just like the rest of all I had of his wasn't mine. But in my need to understand and explain to myself what I was doing, I thought of it all as my inheritance: the last words he wanted her to hear, she wanted me to hear, too. And after everything I had already read in his journals, where he seemed so utterly free in sharing his hopes and shattered dreams, his suicidal ideation and his homicidal fantasies about Stanley Byrd, what more could possibly be divulged that I didn't already know?

I couldn't open it. I couldn't break my sister's hair. Instead, I cut the short edge of the envelope with a razor blade, removing just a tiny sliver of it, leaving the tape and Holly's hair intact. Were Holly to come back to life and look at it she would hardly be able to tell I had opened it all.

William was the king of lists, so I shouldn't have been surprised that the envelope contained another one. Three pages long, on yellowed-lined paper, in the handwriting I'd always admired: his List of Shame. There was almost no commentary, just the facts, one delivered after the other in austere self-flagellation, secrets that he would not, could not even commit to his journals.

I'm not going to list them all here: enough, finally, is enough. But there is this one note he made, a critical moment in his life he may never have told anyone about: "My hero A.J., a scoutmaster," he wrote, sexually assaulted him "in the councilor's tent."

No interpretation or analysis from William; he doesn't even say how old he was, but I would guess eleven or twelve. Presumably they were camping; William was probably going for another badge. This life-altering episode— William turned away from the impact of it himself. William Nealy, the boy with the bright red hair, the bowl cut, the freckles, the nerdy thick glasses, who was claiming his right to be a boy by joining the Scouts, and becoming, one day, a great one, could not face this moment down. What must it have done to him, then and for the rest of his life? How hard is it to hold on to a dream of the man you want to become when the best version you have of that man assaults you while you're sleeping? The emotional energy it took to sustain a dream so corrupted had to have been exhausting, and confusing. He felt trapped, certainly: he could not go backward, because there was nothing there for him. But what lay ahead for him now? Maybe this was his very first real secret, one he kept for his entire life. Had he ever told Holly,

I think she would have told me at some point in the last ten years of her life. Maybe this is when he split himself in two.

But there are no more details from William, no self-examination or reflection. He simply moves on from there: "I stole a pistol from my grandfather when I was 13 and gave it back to him when he was dying, 8 years later . . ."

And on and on: looking through medicine cabinets in friend's bathrooms, "Gil and I dancing in dewy suburban lawns before dawn, naked, when we were 8," making out with a friend's girlfriend, wandering through the forest "scoping out the back trails, the hidey holes, prepping for future adventures, laying faked evidence for bragged-on but uncommitted crimes," followed by pretty straight-forward titillations and teenage misadventures, unwise and provocative but ultimately forgivable.

He was never able to forgive himself, though. The good life he led didn't erase or absolve him or seem to give him any respite from the guilt he felt for his transgressions; the good life he led was, to him, a cover, a ruse, a self to hide his other self beneath. He was quite aware of the image he had created—the Man with No Name who had made a name for himself mapping rivers, climbing mountains, racing down treacherous trails on his mountain bike, and writing books about all of it later. As he wrote more than once in the journals, no one would be able to handle who he really was. If he was the model of the toxic male, he was toxic only to himself, cool on the outside and burning with shame on the inside. These deepest and darkest secrets became the foundation for the creation of a new William, the one everyone knew, and loved, and some of us almost worshipped.

He ends it all like this: "I think this rant may continue until I've put it all out there . . . then I can read it and burn it and eat the ashes." But he never did that. Here were his confessions—his rant, as he put it. He never burned it, though, and most crucially, he never put any of it "out there," where it is now. No one ever knew what happened to him; no one knew why he was the way he was, or why he did what he did. His other self lived and died on the page, as gone as if that part of him had never existed at all—until I found it in a cardboard box in the back of a dark closet and gave it a second life.

Part Three

24 Last Days

No matter how many wonderful things you did, you
will always be remembered for the last one you did
wrong. —William, from *Boyz Life*, an unfinished manuscript

HE'D ALWAYS HEARD voices, faraway siren songs of death, like
music drifting through the woods from the home of a distant neighbor. But when he woke up that morning, out of
a suicidal dream—Sunday, July 15, 2001—it was different:
the voice was in his head now, and the voice was his. Like he
was talking to himself. He wrote this down in his journal,
what he heard, the message he had received: *Imperative . . .
do this, soon.*

Then, as if it was already out of his hands, he wrote:
So so sad.

This is what happened.

Since the week before, he wrote, he'd been absorbed with
the prospect of following through on his lifelong desire to
kill himself. After so many years orbiting his destination
planet, he felt ready to enter that atmosphere—long-desired
but still unknown to him—and touch down. He wished he
could have had more practice. He learned a little from the
first time he tried this, six years ago, but only what *not* to

do. And he'd never done anything in his life without planning for it, without practice, practice, practice. When he was first learning to skate, at forty, he practiced in private for months, where no one could see him, until he got the moves down. Then he went out into the world—a full-fledged skater. If he could have practiced killing himself, he would have, but since that was impossible, he just had to plan and plot and hope for the best. He had guns and drugs and he knew how to use them both. He knew that suicide was not *just* about killing yourself; that's the easy part, and when you do it right it's over in a flash. But there's a lot of prep that goes into it, a lot of paperwork. Let no one tell you different.

I never found his very last journal. I only saw the few pages of it that Holly copied and showed around—his last days. She made dozens of copies and gave them to friends and family. She wanted to show us how crazy what had happened was. How maybe he had been crazy himself toward the end. She wanted to know what we thought of the whole thing.

Or maybe she just didn't want to be the only one who read it, who had to carry this dreadful story around in her head forever.

The last few years of his life William seemed to recede, in person and in his journals as well. It was a gradual thing that happened after the charges against Stanley were dropped.

I rarely saw him. He was agoraphobic, I think. He didn't even want to talk on the telephone. When I visited he'd be in the bedroom, reading, or upstairs in his office trying to draw. Holly, though she had been operated on shoulder to toe, was by far the livelier of the two.

The last two complete journals of his I have focus mostly on the day-to-day. The road his life was on felt smoother now—not happier, really, just less tortured. It reads like he's accepted himself for who he is, and calibrated his desires based on that. He's no longer railing against the world. There's not a lot of noise in them, inside or out. The journals are friendly text-capsules of day-to-day events, with very little commentary, very little complaint. Even stressful moments feel calm. No fears of implosion. No threats to his life or the lives of others. The only truly apocalyptically paranoid entry in the last year of his life is on May 15, 2001, when he wrote about a report he heard on NPR. A national database was being established to detect abuse of oxycontin. "Possibly if Holly started conserving and ceased double-scripting everything would be okay . . . I'm thinking I may need a lot more ammo: 9mm, .30, .357, 12 gauge, 00, etc. We may be getting a visit from the DEA."

But even this—making sure he had enough ammo to hold off the DEA—was written in a less frantic, almost easy-going voice. His asthma was getting worse, as was his back pain. Holly had already had one shoulder replacement and was going to get another soon. Basie, my younger sister Barrie's son, his (our) nephew, was spending a lot of time with them, and many of William's entries describe their visits—"rounding numbers," playing with Legos, killing Nazis. Lots of writing for school.

There was a sense of peace. But I think the peace came from the decision he'd made, this deal he made with himself to die. He'd been on the road to suicide all of his life, but now, from where he was, he could see the end of it. Just a little farther to go.

I looked back at everything I'd read, beginning in 1978:

> Last weekend I felt that I was truly headed for the
> edge. These periods of acute depression seem to
> manifest themselves daily—maybe it's all depression
> interrupted by short daily flights of euphoria that give
> me the impression that I'm sporadically depressed
> instead of sporadically happy.

Followed by innumerable suicidal ideation dreams over the years, his own first botched attempt at dying, his casual one-off observations ("If it weren't for Holly and the pigs, I'd kill myself") to his futile attempts to convince himself that he might be able to avoid it.

> Main complaint—Total alienation, everyone's
> enthusiasm drives me suicidal. I'm just so bloody
> tired, useless . . . the idea of non-being, with eternal
> sleep is so attractive, it's almost a woman/siren . . .
> seducing me.

Even so, he did not give up easily. In January 1996:

> More reasons to live—If I did nothing more than take
> care of Holly, our animals and this beautiful place
> and do my weird art I would be doing great things.
> I can't do everything great, as I seem to demand of
> myself—climb, ski, paddle blade, bike, surf sea and
> sky, draw sculpt, construct, be a naturalist, a neo-abo
> archeological exhibit, geologist, criminalist, writer,
> martial artist, musician, physicist . . .

In the journals now, Edgar Hitchcock and Stanley Byrd seemed to have been quietly subsumed into William's daily life. They'd been folded into his despair. In late December 2000, eight months before he died, he revisited his list of woes, the same ones he'd been writing about in one way or another for twenty years: "slightly paranoid, ashamed of my artwork/career/money situation . . . Ready to give up. Tired of being head bottle washer/houseboy/nurse, etc, etc." Followed a few days later with: "Feeling much better. If I skate every nice day . . . I'll be fine."

But in the back of that same journal, where he taped the cards and wrote the telephone numbers he wanted to remember, he also wrote down Stanley Byrd's date of birth and social security number. Stanley Byrd's DOB and SSN are in *all* of his journals, in fact, from 1995 on.

And all this time, in spite of everything, not a day went by that he didn't make this life they'd made for themselves work. He took Holly's purse to the car when she was leaving, fed the pigs and mended the fences, swept and cleaned and cooked, packed and unpacked, followed the weather reports, learned to skate, rented movies, read books. He took on the responsibility for two lives, and both of them were burdens. It wasn't Holly that weighed him down, though; it was his powerlessness to fix her that did that.

He spent the last two weeks of his life preparing for his death. He made a long list of everything he owned, to be sold or divvied up between family and friends: the van, his artifacts, arrowheads and rocks, musical instruments, insurance. This came to about $25,000. How conscious and conscientious he was about *everything!*—approaching suicide not as a discrete act but as a process that takes careful organization over time. On July 15, in his last journal entry, he wrote *Woke up out of a suicidal dream. Strong S. ideation.* Later that same day, I called Holly and invited her and William to dinner at Chapel Hill's renowned Southern cuisine restaurant, Crook's Corner. Laura was bartending that night. She put herself through the UNC School of Social Work bartending, and though she'd been working full-time as a social worker for a year, she still bartended occasionally. (This was where Laura and I met, in fact, one night by chance when she had been asked to come in to sub, and I decided to eat there, alone, at the bar. Kismet.) Holly said, "Okay, but I doubt William will want to do that." She said he was in bed reading a book about the Boxer Rebellion. The Boxers were members of a Chinese secret society called the

Yihequan, who performed physical exercises they believed would make them able to withstand bullets. He probably wouldn't want to come, she said, but she asked him anyway and he surprised her by saying yes.

We met at the bar at seven. William was at the far end, sitting quietly, while Holly as usual did the talking. I looked past her to William. He wasn't wearing his sunglasses. I saw how glassy his eyes were, recessed, detached. Maybe he was high, I thought at the time. Maybe that was the reason he looked the way he did, but that wasn't it. He just wasn't *there*; he really wasn't there at all. He wasn't listening to a word any of us were saying. He was listening to the voices in his head. He was making his plans over dinner.

Laura thought, later, that he had come out to say goodbye.

On Tuesday, July 17, Holly and William had a Family Picnic, as they did every few weeks, weather permitting. They'd brought all of their animals—Belle the dog, Sherman and Harold (their precious pot-bellied pigs), all of their box turtles and snapping turtles and snakes and bunnies, and gone to a spot near New Hope Creek, at the edge of their twenty acres, not too far from their house. One of the snapping turtles William had found right after it had been born, when it still had a piece of eggshell on it. He loved them, so primitive, like little dinosaurs. Sherman, Harold, and Belle would follow them down to the creek; Holly would be on her scooter. With the turtles and snakes in terrariums and the rabbit in its little cage, they spread the blanket beneath the oaks and pine and ate cheese and crackers. "We tried to have a little Garden of Eden moment," Holly said.

It was a good day. He'd told her that tomorrow he was going to release them all, all the turtles and snakes and bunnies, because the weather was good and the chances that they could survive on their own were better now.

The Family Picnic, she reported, was perfect.

The next morning Holly left for the hospital. She had doctors' appointments all day long. Truly: at any given moment you could look at these two remarkable people and be amazed at what they'd been through together, and yet here they were, still standing. William's body had kept his spirit afloat all these years; Holly's spirit had kept her body going. This was like a race to see which would go first.

He took her purse to the car, the white Lincoln sedan they'd just gotten back from the mechanic, and he gave the pigs their breakfast—an entire box of Cheerios. She was pulling out of the drive when she stopped and rolled down the window.

"Oh," she said. "I keep forgetting to tell you. The car runs so much better now."

He turned from the pigs and he said to her, "It god damn well ought to! We just spent a thousand dollars on it."

Out of all the words there are in the world, these were the last ones she ever heard him speak. To him, they must have seemed ideal: no sappy long loving looks goodbye. No tell-tale *I love you, baby*. Just business as usual. She didn't suspect a thing.

But as soon as her car was out of sight, he began his final preparations.

He set the animals free.

He wrote his first note.

And two hours later he was on his way. Today was the day.

July 18th, 2001. Late afternoon.

By July 18, 2001, Laura and I had been living together for a month.

There was a message on our answering machine that day from William.

Hey brother. This is William. [Pause] *Holly and I had a little fight.* [Pause] *You probably want to go over to her house—our house—and be with her. I'm going up to the houseboat. Okay. Bye.*

Such a bizarre message.

And what a mistake this was for him, calling me.

Had he not called me, all the arrangements he had made for his death would have gone off without a hitch. Because otherwise it was meticulously thought through: one, to ensure its success, and two, to protect Holly, inasmuch as he could protect her from the worst day of her life. He would do it far away from home so she wouldn't be the first to find him. He would even leave a note in his van to have whoever found him call *me*, and not her, so she could hear it first from me. But he didn't really think this part through, otherwise he would have known that as soon as I heard the message on my machine, I'd call Holly, and that, from there, everything—his entire game plan—would unravel.

I'm going to kill myself, he might well have said, *and this is where I'm going to do it.*

When Laura came home shortly thereafter, I had her listen to the message. At first, she didn't think it was all that odd.

But I persisted, picking it apart. Why would he say *This is William?* I would know who it was from the very first word. Why would he call to tell me they were having a fight? And why would *I* need to be with Holly after *their* fight?

Still I couldn't say aloud what I was thinking: *I wonder if he's going to the houseboat to kill himself.* It was like the way it was in Birmingham when everyone knew that Edgar was dead but no one could say it, because saying it seemed to make it so. Saying so made it real.

We played the message over and over on speakerphone. *This is William . . . had a little fight . . . You probably want to . . . be with her.* And that stumble: *Her house.*

It took me an hour or more to get in touch with Holly. Her ringer had been off or the phone was at the bottom of her purse, and the cellphone was new to her and it really wasn't something she used all that often and sometimes forgot to even look at.

By the time I connected with her, she was at home. She'd brought back a bunch of Thai food for dinner. She wore wrist braces, used a cane of course, and rode a scooter to go longer distances. Sometimes she and William would take the scooter to a parking lot, and he'd tie himself to the back of it and get pulled along on his skates.

I asked her how she was. Fine, she said. Tired, but fine. Hungry. Her voice was upbeat, even chipper. Not unusual for her: she was, despite everything, a naturally happy person. She did not sound like she and William had been through an earth-shattering argument, one so upending he actually called to tell me about it.

"William's not there?" I said, probing.

"Nope," she said. "I thought he would be. I don't know where he got to. Maybe there's a note somewhere."

"Did you have a fight?"

"A fight?" She thought about it, laughed. "Not that I know of. Why?"

"He called me," I said. "He left a message on the phone. He said you had a fight and that he'd gone to the houseboat."

"No," she said. Then I could almost hear her mind going over the day, running through it all, yesterday, the day before, to see if there was anything to remember. "Nothing happened."

"Why would he say that?"

She was quiet. When she spoke again her voice was softer.

"I don't know. Maybe he . . . I don't know."

"I just wonder why he called me at all."

That was the thing, the inescapable weirdness of the fact of the call.

"I don't know," she said. And then she seized on the narrative that would pull us all through the rest of the day and night. "But I bet it's a bender."

William had quit drinking and smoking years ago: these last years were all about nonalcoholic beer, chewing tobacco, and Nicorettes. But once a year or so he'd fall off the wagon. He'd usually wait until Holly was out of town, and then spend a weekend deeply involved in getting back in touch with the self he knew so well and hated so much. Just throw himself into it and come out the other side and be smoke-free and sober for another year or so.

"I should go up there," she said.

"Why?"

"In case he falls off the houseboat and hits his head and drowns." She laughed. "There's a bar up there full of townies and rednecks and slutty-looking women."

"The kind he likes."

"Exactly." Laughing. She'd made her decision. "I'm going to drive up there."

"Really?"

"I think I'll drive up and see what's going on. Bring the Thai food."

"Do you want me to go with you?"

This was what I said. This was what I'm almost sure I said. *Do you want me to go with you?* But it was the way

219 THIS ISN'T GOING TO END WELL 219

you'd offer to do something you didn't *really* want to do; a kind offer, semi-sincere, but one you hoped wasn't necessary. I think I was hoping that she would say no, even though I knew she should say yes. I was able to convince myself that this was okay because, as I have said, I have a talent for compartmentalizing.

She said no. "He'd be embarrassed if I brought you with me. He gets kind of loopy-drunk and silly. And dumb."

Here is where I should have said, wish I had said, *I'm going with you,* because I think she might have let me come. Had I persisted, she would have had to insist I *not* come, and I would have believed her that there was nothing out of the ordinary about this at all, that it was just that time of year for him. She'd go up, take care of him, make sure he made it back to the other side.

"So you'll call me and let me know what's going on?"

She said she would.

I let her go without me.

She called again when she got to the houseboat. By this time, it was around nine-thirty. It was fully night, dark in the empty marina.

"He's not here," she said. "But he's been here."

"How do you know?"

She laughed. "Because there are about a dozen empty beer cans and a pack of cigarettes in the boat."

Her suspicions were correct: William was on a bender. She went into town to look for him, hoping she would find

him at a bar; she didn't. Exhausted, she said she was going
to sleep on the houseboat, hoping he might return there by
morning.

There was no desperation in her voice, no worry or concern at all. I couldn't hold back.

"I hate to even say this," I said to her. "But do you think
that he might have hurt himself?"

She didn't pause long enough to blink. "No," she said.
"I don't—no. Things are good. He's been good. We've just
been . . . swimming along lately. And this past week he's
seemed great."

Swimming along.

What was it like that night, alone at the lake in the dark?
No one else was there, not a soul. All the boats empty, the
lake's gently rolling water knocking their hulls against the
pylons. Otherwise, silence. A bird called. A deer snapping a
twig, the sound carrying over the water. The starlight was
sharper, pointed, somehow newer, less worn, than it was in
town, where the light seems used, tarnished. I believed her
when she told me she didn't think he would hurt himself.
But I thought back to a few nights before, when we were
sitting at the bar. When his eyes had looked like they had an
amphibian's third lid.

She walked down the docks, looking in every boat with
a flashlight. He might have tripped and stumbled into one
of them, passed out or fallen.

She had brought a book. She always brought a book

everywhere she went. We talked about it once, how you always want to have a book in case your car breaks down or you get kidnapped. But before she arranged the pillows on the bench in the houseboat, the bench with the thinly padded covering, something occurred to her. *Maybe he's in the van.* Why had this not occurred to her? It was possible he had passed out in the van. He could have slipped through the parking lot and slithered inside and fallen asleep.

So, one more time that night, she left the boat and, cane in hand, stepped off the rickety dock and walked up the broken asphalt to the van. She looked in the driver's side window and even though it was dark she could see that he wasn't there, not in the front seat at least. She couldn't see in the back. She tried to open the door but it was locked, as was the door on the passenger side, as were the gated doors at the back. She knocked and slammed her cane against the doors and called out *"William, William!"* Her voice echoed all the way across the parking lot and to the lake and across the lake into the woods. He would have heard her had he been there. He would have awoken. He wasn't there though and she called to tell me this, and then she walked back to the boat and went to sleep, and so did we.

The morning light woke her, and she called me as she was walking toward his van. I could hear her walking, shoes crunching gravel. My heart was beating so fast. I was living in this moment, the same way an audience member, watching a film, was living in the moment of the film, watching the characters interact, the plot unwinding, there and not there at the same time.

"I'm at the van," she said.

Her voice trailed off and she was quiet for a moment.

"Holly?"

She was already in shock, I think. Her voice was flat.

"I'm looking in the window. There's a note. It's on a pad of paper, on that thing that sticks to the dashboard. You know. It says, 'My name is William Nealy. Please call Daniel Wallace'"—giving my phone number—"'as soon as you read this. I'm behind the office building.'" She paused. Then she finished reading the note. "'A copy of my DNR is in the glove compartment.'"

Her voice was steady, even, uninflected, as if she were reading a grocery list.

"Holly? Does it say anything else?"

But she didn't answer me. She took a deep, sharp intake of breath—not because there was anything else to read, because there wasn't—but to let the moment pass through her, I imagine, the precise moment her life was halved into the before and the after.

25 His Notes

WHEN WILLIAM ARRIVED at the marina that afternoon, he gathered all the things he would need that night and headed down to the houseboat and settled in. He was well-lubricated by now, full of pharmaceuticals and beer, chain-smoking, listening to the voice in his head, which as he said was his voice now, which it had been all week while he'd been planning his demise side-by-side with his lifelong partner. Somehow, he was still able to compose the notes he had to write—one to his mother and one to Holly. He needed to explain how he got here, down the long road of his life to this place. Because it's a long road. And everything argues against death. Life argues against it, even when life is what you think you want to escape, even when life itself appears to be the problem. But this had been William's struggle since the beginning. He was most alive when he was closest to death.

Note #1

William wrote three suicide notes on the last day of his life—thirteen total pages. I have all of them, because Holly made photocopies and gave them to me.

The first note he wrote that morning, right after Holly left for the hospital, after he set the animals free.

He seemed to be laying the groundwork—not just for the suicide to come, but for the future notes themselves, as if a preface were necessary. Or you could look at it as warming up, prewriting, getting into the mood. That first one was lost in a stack of mail, though, so Holly didn't see it when he thought she would—when she came home from the hospital. She didn't see it for another week, long after she saw the other ones.

I imagine he wrote it sitting in the booth in their kitchen. They'd always loved diners, and the movie *Diner*, with Kevin Bacon, was one of their favorites, and they'd built a reproduction of a diner booth in their kitchen. The Formica table, the red vinyl-covered seats on either side, the mustard and ketchup silos, an art-deco lamp suspended above it. They even had a tiny jukebox. This was where William would have been when he wrote the note—a clean, well-lighted place.

He explained that his back and his knees had been hurting so much that he had been pilfering oxycontins from her "stash," and knew he had to stop. But he just couldn't.

"I can't spend the rest of my life in rehab," he wrote. "You have no idea how horrid I feel right now, what this will do to you in the future. So I'm running away."

Then this. Oh, this, this recognition of the impossible life that has been made for him to live. "Maybe I'll whack Stanley . . . Maybe I'll drive into a tree."

Stanley, to the very last day.

"I'll hole up, write some more letters to you and to Ma, think think think . . . try to figure this thing out, try to find a way out." But there's really no more thinking to be done along these lines; his mind was made up. "I'm doing what I've got to do to protect you from what I've become . . . I barely know myself anymore."

Then: "God, I love you. Forgive me. More later."

And a PS: "Please don't call the cops or anything . . . you may want to call Daniel tonite."

Note #2

Dear Ma,

When you read this I'll be gone.

William's note to his mother, Louise Nealy, is five handwritten pages long. In it he wrote about the back pain, the asthma, the hopelessness. He wrote about how, when he was eleven or twelve years old, he made a promise to himself that if his asthma ever got bad again he would "never experience the little deaths chronic asthma brings on." This is exactly what was happening now, he wrote. His asthma was back. If he was going to honor this promise he made to the boy he was over thirty-five years ago, he would have to kill himself now.

"The last year or so I feel certain I've begun showing signs of COPD [chronic obstructive pulmonary disease]. Nowadays I'm getting the asthma attacks from simply jogging up the ten yards from our parking area." And: "Please don't blame yourself or Holly for this . . . it's my doing and it's been my doing all along. I've had a good life it's just turning out to be a short life . . . I've been loved by you and Holly more than any human being ever deserved."

Much of the note is spent encouraging his mother to leave Holly alone. "Let her go her way after this. If I were her, me and my family would be a painful memory . . . Forgive me and let Holly live her life."

He wrote things to his mother that he wrote nowhere else. He admitted that "it's going to be hard and awful for her, losing 50 percent of her life support system." This may be the truest thing he ever said. He knew what the consequences of his death were going to be. "Doing this is not the hardest thing I've ever done in my life, but knowing the pain I'm going to cause is."

"I'm so sorry to have done this awful thing," he wrote to her, still at least an hour away from doing the awful thing. And reading it I want to say, *It's not too late. It hasn't happened yet.*

Stop.

Note #3

The note to Holly. Eight pages long, dated "Thursday, 5pm."

"Just arrived at the houseboat," he began. "It's in better shape than I'd imagined."

There had been times, after being off the boat for a couple of months, they would come back and find it full of bugs or taking on water. I have a couple of their lake journals, and they are, like his private journals, very detailed, the kind of detail he liked, describing the world, what things looked like and how they worked, and his knowledge of it all. He called Holly "Captain Holly" when she guided the boat out into the water, and she wrote in the journal, too, in a voice so distinctly hers. "There is a weird little bug that sounds like a strong person using castanets, but William says it's some kind of cricket." Just the two of them, alone, with their little dog Belle, immersed in the experience of being the two of them.

What a comfort it had been for him, he wrote, to be in this "loving space" they created. For two people who had created their own ecosystem, their own world, this boat and this lake was an expansion of their territory. He admitted that there was no explanation he could ever give that would justify "this terrible thing." But then he tried to justify it. His back pain topped the list, followed by "the loss of function/energy/joy" he'd felt in the last year. The list of ailments did not end there. "My cholesterol is bad, I'm a drug addict, I've got COPD and emphysema, I'm a depressed neurotic or a neurotic depressed person . . . all of it self-inflicted." He must have focused on this list constantly in the last few weeks, day after day, like memorizing an argument, a debate with life itself.

He revisited the promise he made to his eleven-year-old self here—the promise "that I would never experience the little deaths chronic asthma brings on ever again." But he smoked pot and cigarettes and cigars for decades, and coming full circle with his self-fulfilling prophecy, here he was "wheezing and smoking Marlboros." Which was only further proof that he was making the right decision.

It all made perfect sense.

This was followed by the list he'd been working on and thinking about for the last few days: who would get his guns, fishing equipment and knives, his arrowheads and artifacts, his slingshots and "oriental fighting sticks," and the hundreds and hundreds of dollars she might be able to make if she put his boating stuff on eBay and sold it "to whitewater necrophiliacs." And who owed him money, and the balance on his Visa Gold—$3500.

It's so sad. It's the saddest thing I've ever read in my life. How could it not be? Are there good/better/best ways to spend the last few minutes of the life you're allowing yourself? Watching the sunset, rescuing a kitten from a tree? Does it make any real difference if you're drunk or high at this point, or if you're imagining a future world without you in it in which your widow is posting photographs on eBay of *Kayak belonging to cartooning legend William Nealy?*

"As awful as this is, your beauty and infinite capacity for love-giving kept my head above water for thirty years. I'm not the person I used to be but you as usual are ascending to the highest levels of human possibility." Which was a little sentimental coming from him, so much so that he had to state parenthetically: "I'm not being cynical . . . this is me on pills being mushy, or trying to be."

• • •

Holly and William had spent their lives looking for ways to be alone, but alone *together*. The rest of the world only presented problems for them to overcome. They traveled the country together. They settled in Chapel Hill, where they didn't know a soul. Then they made some friends in town, so he built them a house in the middle of nowhere, but nowhere wasn't far enough away. So they'd gotten this boat and spent nights out on the water, reading and writing and fishing, in a place where they couldn't be found. They really didn't need the rest of us. Everything that had to be done in the world, William did; all the fixing of things, the naming of things, the taking care of things, the saving of my sister's life. The creation of all the mechanics that kept the wheels of life moving so Holly could be happy in it. And in return, she saved his. It was Holly who brought the beauty, the laughter, the spirit, the hope. The reasons.

All of that gone now. William was all alone, all by himself.

"I love you so much!" he wrote, and he signed it, as he signed everything to her, "Me."

Then he put the gun in his backpack and walked into the woods behind the marina office, where she would find him later.

Part Four

"One day I'm going to write a book about William's mind, or somebody is . . ." —Holly, interview with the *Independent*, March 2002

26 Polio Creek

WILLIAM RAN HIS first river when he was twelve years old and he almost died doing it. It wasn't *really* a river, though. It was a suburban creek that ran through his backyard in Birmingham, a creek that, in his words, "had been engineered, channelized and civilized, walled on both sides eight feet high, first with sandstone, then with concrete." They called it "Polio Creek," because that's what his parents told him he would get if he ever got in it. But the creek went everywhere, zigzagging through his neighborhood, and there were tunnels connecting it to other neighborhoods. You could walk for miles on it when the water level was low, but occasionally after a big rain there would be a flash flood, and the water would rise eight or nine feet, and suddenly there was a river raging through his backyard "like a limbless Godzilla."

He wrote an essay about it—illustrated, of course, and beautifully written, evoking all the joys and fears of a childhood adventure.

He had a boat, "a plastic rowboat-looking affair from K-Mart that also served as a wading pool, turtle pond or sled," and one day in 1965 he got in it and slipped into the watery behemoth. "Polio Creek shot past the breach with a low sucking moan, and as I cleared the wall I was snatched downstream. This was like some demented new ride at the state fair—Mad Mouse with no breaks and no end, an insane machine. I was falling down a shaft with walls of concrete, water and air."

As it whipped him around successive ninety-degree bends and his boat took on water, he realized what was about to happen: "I am going to drown today."

He did not drown that day. But the experience created a blueprint for the kind of life he wanted to live: that a day not spent close to Death, preferably on or near the water, was a day lost forever.

In *Urban Birds*, Edgar Hitchcock's unpublished 1985 novella, an accountant named Peter Malcolm becomes entangled in a drug-related murder of a friend and client named Archie. Malcolm knows what happened, but unfortunately gets struck by lightning and loses his short-term memory. His best friend is a mysterious fellow by the name of Phearson McLiesh, who is "just about everything Peter Malcolm was not. Mac was meek. McLiesh smirked at authority. McLiesh was cool in all situations. Mac was not . . . Phearson McLiesh could hold his liquor and Mac couldn't. Mac was gullible and plodding. Mcliesh was cynical and conniving."

But they are both called Mac.

We never meet Phearson McLiesh, because it turns out Malcolm and McLiesh are one and the same. Mac creates his fictional counterpart in the army, in order to get close to a woman, but over the years Malcolm notes that McLiesh had grown "in importance and dimension. He now had a multi-faceted personality of his own."

I don't know if William ever read this story. But if he did I suspect he would have recognized Malcolm's dilemma as his own, in the same way he recognized Princess Caraboo as his soul sister from 150 years ago.

But how did Edgar come up with the character at all, one so close to the reality of his real-world best friend, William Nealy? It wouldn't have been like William to share his predicament with Edgar—that's not the sort of emotional information he shared with anybody—and yet, at the same time, I can't accept the idea that the Malcolm/Nealy parallel is pure happenstance.

This makes me wonder about the nature of *influence*. It's so mysterious. Can we ever know why we are who we are—the recipe that makes us the unique, bewildering, beautiful and sometimes insane creatures we end up becoming? I think it's possible that influence can occur tacitly, by an invisible hand—like a contact high. I think the invention of Peter Malcolm was what happened with William and Edgar, and what happened with me: I absorbed their secret selves without knowing it, in a kind of mysterious osmosis, and became who I am because of it. We're unknowable even to ourselves because of the unknown influences that shape us, like underground rivers flowing through our souls, unseen.

William, the outcast weakling with the distant, alcoholic father and the unhinged, lonely, God-obsessed mother, turned into a smarter, stronger, and more competent man than he ever had a reason to be. Why? Even he could never understand it. He lived his life on mountains, rivers, trees, and in caves, saving lives, making art—living the life of a good man, if not a great one—in order to live as far away from his broken self as possible, to succeed in the outside world when he couldn't with the one inside of him. If he had died in his sleep on July 17, one day before he had planned to kill himself, he would probably be a family saint.

That difference is no difference to me anymore, although it's taken me these last four years to be able to say that. He *was* like Odysseus. Heroic and destructive. Cursed by the gods to be himself, he stayed alive anyway. He wrote ten books. He built a home. He took care of my sister for thirty years. Then he devastated her.

I'm not his obvious heir. I am almost embarrassed at how far from the mark I fall from inheriting his very best qualities. My thirst for adventure is easily quenched, indoors or out. He lived his life on the edge of a razor; I live mine writing stories on a hotel-room bed. I quit taking serious drugs the day Len Bias died, on June 19, 1986, a man I never even knew. He was a basketball player for the University of Maryland and was drafted by the Boston Celtics with the second overall pick in the 1986 draft. He died two days later of cardiac arrhythmia induced by cocaine. I had watched him play for years and admired his mind and skills and strength, his Jordan-like hops and play-making abilities. He died as all his dreams were coming true, and for some reason his story (I still don't know why, quite) scared me straight. No hard drugs anymore. I still drink. I've smoked too many cigarettes in my life. I'm usually in bed by midnight. *You take such small bites*, a friend once told me. True. But I get to live the rest of my life with my great love. I'm not in the world to break it or to be broken by it, to challenge it, to beat the odds.

Still, I wish I had inherited just a little more.

We live and die by the lights of the stories we tell about ourselves. They can both sustain us and sink us. Edgar and William died the way they always pretended they had wanted to—in explosively romantic and anti-romantic ways—and for the rest of us it's supposed to be heartbreaking, and it is.

But William is not bedridden now, or in an asylum; Edgar is not wasting away in prison. The hopeful reader might think I'm setting the bar far too low for two such remarkable people. Are these really their only possibilities—murder or prison, suicide or asylum? Yes, probably. I think so. They did not have that many options, and they were not the kind to wait and see.

But I'm the wait-and-see type, I think. I want to live to be old, or older anyway, and see what happens next. There are so many ways to die. There's murder, of course, and suicide, and as much as I would like to think these are endings I can avoid, there appear to be no safe places left in the world, on our streets or in our hearts. They're the darker options, clearly, but they're options available to us all. My mother accidentally stepped in a trash can, fell, and broke her neck; my father's heart exploded; my cousin died of AIDS; Holly's diseased body fell apart. But I look both ways, twice, when I cross the street, as if this is going to make all the difference. Every minute of life is a reckoning; an ending just as awful if not worse may be waiting for me out there—my death, the only experience in my life I will never be able to write about. Without William I wouldn't be who I am, but I am not him, which is a blessing. Without William I would be something wholly different, possibly unrecognizable, a distant relative of myself—writing invoices instead of novels. And though I can't imagine what my life would be like if I *weren't* a writer, being one is, in a way, not like living at all. On a dark and stormy night, a writer arrives at a way station between experience and understanding, and really never leaves it. But writing is better than living, in one way at least: there are an infinite number of opportunities to correct your worst mistakes.

Epilogue

Thanksgiving

SOMETIME IN THE year before he died, William made me a small leather pouch, the kind of pouch I imagine a prospector might have worn tied to his belt, something to store the small pieces of gold he surely found. In the pouch he made me were half a dozen miniature screwdrivers. There were flathead screwdrivers and Phillips-head screwdrivers, one for almost every kind of screw, small or large. I'd just bought a house and a homeowner needed such things, he said. By 2019 the screwdrivers were scattered in drawers throughout the house, or lost, but I still had the empty pouch, hanging by the leather lace you tightened to close it. For some reason we had it hanging from a hook on our refrigerator. It had been there for years.

I mention it now because in 2019 Laura and I had been invited to spend Thanksgiving in Maryland, at a place called Mineral Springs Farm. Seven years before he died, in 1990, my father had purchased the farm; his second wife, Ruth Noble Groom, lives there still. Mineral Springs Farm is forty-five acres of land on the Eastern Shore, with a main house by the bay, stables with real horses, a barn that had been beautifully renovated into a two-story guest house with two bedrooms, a billiard table, a kitchen, and a library, as well as the taxidermied heads and bodies of ten or twelve formerly wild animals, including a fox, a deer, an ox, ducks, and a tiger. A hundred yards away from the barn was another small house that was being rented to someone I didn't know and never met. To me it felt more like a compound than a farm, but whatever it is, it's beautiful and pastoral in ways that are beyond my powers to describe, like walking through the imagination of someone with good taste and a whole lot of money.

Laura and I were there along with my daughter, Lillian, and her husband, Ryan, and Rangeley's family. Rangeley's family stayed at an inn—there were eight of them in her entourage, too many even for a compound—and the rest of us stayed in the barn.

In a glade between the main house and the barn is a graveyard. It's been there since the mid-nineteenth century. You can just barely make out the dates on the small marble headstones, all the edges worn soft, not quite upright anymore, sinking into the earth, even the names weathered away. Those graves are enclosed inside a short white picket fence. Outside the fence where the wild fields start, pets are buried, six or seven or eight of them. Peacocks stroll brightly through the woods, appearing and disappearing, here and gone.

There are other graves, too, and they're more recent. My father is buried there. That was in 1997. I was thirty-eight years old. His ashes were placed in a golden box, and at his funeral, attended by hundreds of people from all over the world, I was tasked with setting the box into the shallow grave. I was a real mess, sobbing, overwhelmed, adjusting the box, turning it one way and then the other, getting it so that it looked and felt just right to me. This was something I really wanted to get right. Once I did that, or gave up trying, I stepped out of the grave and we buried the box and then threw all of our china into the bay. This is a thing the Greeks used to do, apparently.

Holly is there. Friends of my father and Ruth Noble and of her third husband, Robin, are buried in this graveyard, too, all marked by bronze markers on marble slabs.

My father's marker says:

In Loving Memory
Eron Daniel Wallace
June 14, 1930–March 18, 1997
THE ORIGIN
Strong and True

Holly is buried next to my father.

In Memoriam
Holland Lucille Wallace
April 19, 1954–April 1, 2011
Bold, Beautiful, Bright
"Tell me what it is you plan to do with
Your one wild and precious life?"
                              —Mary Oliver

Here is where the ashes I sent to Rangeley are buried, when I was trying to get them as far away as possible from William. In this, if nothing else, I had succeeded.

It was Laura's idea. In early November, weeks before the trip to Maryland she said, "You know, you could do something for William when we're there."

"Like what?"

She sort of shrugged. "I don't know. Have a little service?"

That was all she said, and I knew she was right, and I started imagining right then what I could do, how I could do it, what a service like that might entail.

William had collected arrowheads. He had dozens, many of them in a glass display box with explanatory notes beneath them: the tribe that made them, the years they might have been made. He actually made some arrowheads himself, using the same methods the Native Americans did. This would be something to put in the pouch, but I didn't have a single arrowhead of his. So I ordered two dozen arrowheads from a dealer on eBay, and I put two of them in the pouch: one for William, and one for Holly.

I didn't have the flattened nickel necklaces they'd worn anymore. But there's a train track not far from where we live, in Carrboro. The tracks are in a gulley behind an old mill that's been turned into a mall, and a few times a week a train comes through. A few days before we left for Maryland, I scuttled down the dirt embankment and set the nickels on the track, then I went home. I came back the next day and the nickels were in the gravel between two railroad ties; the rumble of the approaching train had shaken them off. This time I taped them to the track, and the next day went back to get them. They were flatter than a dime. I put those in the pouch with the arrowheads. I put a picture of Holly and William in there, too, and a page from his mother's memory book, of William learning to write his name, *William Nealy, William Nealy*, eight times down the page. I took two strands of Holly's hair from the envelope that had been sealed with them and placed these in the pouch as well.

In our backyard in Chapel Hill, we have a little graveyard of our own. Two of our dogs are buried back there, and Lou, one of our cats. William is there, too, of course, not buried but scattered like dandelion bristles. I willed myself to believe he was still back there, lingering in the soil, some sort of molecular residue of the man he once was, invisible to the eye but real nonetheless. Science would tell me that's true. I found an old, rusty trowel and scooped up some of the dirt, and I placed a teaspoon of it in the pouch. I put the rest of the dirt in a small Tupperware container, and I snapped the lid on tight. I know all the feelings were there, somewhere—the sadness and regret and the shame. And the love. I had a sense of them being there, anyway, but I don't know if I felt them. I don't know that I felt anything at all. What it felt like was a story I was writing, one in which I was Daniel Wallace watching Daniel Wallace as he approached the end of the story, still in that place between experience and understanding.

Laura and I left on the twenty-sixth, spent two days at Rangeley's canal house in Rehoboth, and on the last Thursday in November drove the two hours to Mineral Springs Farm.

Thanksgiving Day was clear and bitterly cold, with the wind off the bay that bit at your skin. We ate oysters and drank wine and then twenty of us—my family and a dozen of Ruth Noble's friends—gathered to eat at five circular tables. There were toasts. Mine was thanking Ruth Noble, whose heart I said was big enough "to hold the living and the dead." And then we ate and drank and visited the horses and played pool and went to bed.

We held the service the next day. Ruth Noble, Robin, Jim, Rangeley, Lillian, Ryan, and Laura were there. I gave each of them an arrowhead, and a little of the dirt from our backyard. I read the poem, "the lesson of the moth," the same poem William read at Edgar's funeral.

> it is better to be happy
> for a moment
> and be burned up with beauty
> than to live a long time
> and be bored all the while

It was a moment, all of us coming together to mourn and remember both Holly and William, and even Edgar, in a way. I don't think this had ever happened before.

But earlier that morning I'd gone to the graveyard by myself. The sun hadn't been up all that long. I was shivering. I found the spot I wanted to bury the pouch, between Holly's grave and my father's, a spot covered in glowing moss and dead brown leaves. I couldn't name what it was, this ball of string inside me, but not all feelings are nameable, some may be beyond language, and trying to reduce them to a single word diminishes them. Then I heard a sound behind me and turned.

It was a peacock. But it wasn't like the others, or like any peacock I had ever seen. It was completely white. Every bit of it. The feathers around its long neck were small and delicate and looked as soft as hair. She was one of the most beautiful things I had ever seen. She eased past me and sort of waded into the graveyard, where she stopped, turned, and looked at me. She didn't move, I didn't move. She had joined me in this nameless moment outside of time.

All this reminded me of another death.

A few weeks after Laura's mother Ellen died, a Carolina wren, a female, appeared in our living room. The doors of the house were closed, the windows, too; we had no idea how she'd gotten in. She was perched on a branch of the seven-foot-tall tree we'd inherited from Ellen, which we'd just transplanted into a giant pot. Laura was lying on the daybed beneath the tree, saw the wren, and tried to shoo her out through the back door.

Instead, the wren flew to a basket of navel oranges on the dining room table. The last weeks of Ellen's life, all she would eat were oranges. She would peel one after the other until her little wooden kitchen table was covered in scraps of orange. That's when Laura called for me, and the moment I walked into the room the wren flew from the oranges to a first edition of my first book, *Big Fish*, on a shelf on the other side of the room.

The wren's flight plan seemed very specific. Finally, she flew toward our sun-bright bay window and landed on the sash beneath it, a few inches from the floor. And she didn't move. She was completely still. She looked like she was waiting for something, or for someone, so I walked over to her, kneeled, and reached for her.

And I picked her up. She let me pick her up. I held her feathery warmth in my hands. She didn't flutter a wing. We could see a little round eye looking at us between my fingers. Then I took the bird outside, opened my hands, and we watched her fly away. She flew into the forest behind our house and disappeared.

By this time, both of us were in tears. Ellen had told Laura that when she died she would come back as a bird. She would come back as a bird just to let Laura know that everything was okay, not to worry, I love you. So the wren's apparently magical presence in our living room, and the message it seemed to be sending to us, was extraordinary.

To this day Laura believes that wren was her mother, in the same way, I suppose, that I should believe the snow-white peacock watching me in the graveyard was Holly, or William, or maybe even both.

But I didn't. I didn't believe in people coming back as birds, or as ghosts, or that their souls were in a heaven looking down on us, or that after life there is any sort of life at all. If I could believe that, I thought, I had to believe in everything else, an afterlife full of sentimental spirits who, if they could come back as birds, could come back as anything: the wind, our dog, a pair of old shoes. I thought that if I bought into this idea, I would have to believe in God, or *a* god, and all the other fantastical stories we tell ourselves to give our lives the meaning we think they need. After everything that had happened to me and the people I love, and the death, injustice, and pointless suffering all of us everywhere have endured and will continue to endure, that was something I wasn't interested in doing.

Look at me that morning, though. See me the way the peacock did. I was on my knees, shivering in the cold. I had William's leather pouch, Holly's hair, a piece of paper he wrote his name on, but everything else was fake, a fiction. There were arrowheads in the pouch, but they weren't *his* arrowheads. I had two train-flattened nickels, but Holly and William had never worn them. And if William was anywhere in this Tupperware full of dirt, it would take a spectrometer to find him. But I believed in it anyway, on my knees in the graveyard, trembling. I believed in the mystery.

Holly was there, William was there, I was there. Everyone was finally together. In that moment I believed that an act of kindness could right the world, and not forgive, necessarily, because forgiveness isn't necessary, but absolve us all. And I was sorry, sorry for keeping them apart for so long, and I said so, to the stones and the dirt and to the peacock, who seemed to be listening.

Then I picked up the trowel and started digging.

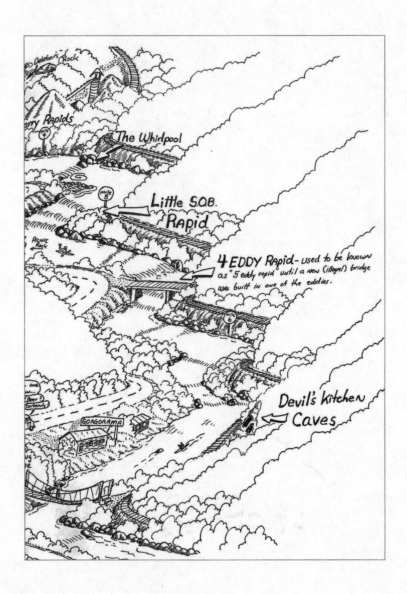

ACKNOWLEDGMENTS

This Isn't Going to End Well is about four people: my sister Holly, my brother-in-law William, our good friend Edgar Hitchcock, and me. I interviewed dozens of people to help tell our stories: my family, friends, friends of friends, lawyers, accountants, some former drug dealers, and one former United States senator. Thanks to you all for allowing me into your lives. Writing a book is like wearing a badge: it gives you the excuse to do so many things you wouldn't do otherwise, and one of them is asking people questions you would never, ever ask them under normal circumstances. You should try it. It's fun.

My dear friend Randall Garrett Kenan loved this book before I'd written the first word of it. Then I wrote it, and he read an almost-nearly-final draft, and said he loved it still. He died at the end of the first COVID-19 summer, August 2020, at the age of fifty-seven; in other words, just a baby. The book is dedicated to him in part because he was its indefatigable cheerleader, but also because it's an opportunity to celebrate him again as the fantastic friend and writer he was. I will never stop celebrating him.

Thank you especially: Barrie Wallace, Rangeley Wallace, Abby Brown, Lillian Hoover, Nic Brown, Alan Shapiro, Elizabeth Woodman, Katherine Sandoz, Elisabeth Benfey, Jamie Chambliss, Steve Troha, Stephanie Elizondo Griest, Gaby Calvocoressi, Bob Sehlinger and Molly Merkle and everyone at Adventure Keen Communications, the Institute of Arts and Humanities at the University of North Carolina, Ani Ibarra, Molly Jernigan, David Madison, Kate Geis, Tom Mallon, Joy Goodwin, Jeff Polish (who let me tell a version of this story at his wonderful storytelling venue, the Monti), Steven Petrow, Whit Rummel, Leslie Frost, Hillary Fisher, and Susanne Freytag. I'm sure I'm missing someone. Double thanks to Christine Pride, a brilliant writer, reader, editor, and friend; I don't know where I would be now, as a writer, without her. And eternal thanks to everyone at Algonquin: Kathy Pories, Travis Smith, Chris Stamey, Brunson Hoole, and everyone else who worked so hard on this book. Kathy Pories edited my very first novel when I was just a thirty-nine-year-old kid in red high-top Chuck Taylors, worn-out jeans, and a thrift store T-shirt. Now that I'm old and wearing wing tips, dark wool suits, and monogrammed cufflinks pretty much all the time, she is my editor again. Thank you, Kathy.

Laura, my wife, has a wide range of superpowers and is essential for just about everything. For this book she was not only a reader but also a witness and participant to the story I was writing. Her perspective and memories and support were invaluable. She deserves a parade.

This Isn't Going to End Well was assembled and written at the O. Henry Hotel, in Greensboro, North Carolina. Some of it was also written at the MacDowell Colony, the Atlantis Lodge in Pine Knoll Shores, NC, and at home. But most of it was written at a hotel an hour away from my front door.

The O. Henry is the only hotel in the world named after a short story writer (the nom de plume of William Sydney Porter, who was born in Greensboro in 1862). It's more than just a name, though, it's an idea the owners, Dennis and Nancy Quaintance, committed to fully when they built it. Portions of O. Henry's most famous story, "The Gift of the Magi," are printed high across the lobby walls beneath the grand vaulted ceiling in what must be 80-point font. The brass trim in the hardwood-lined elevators lists the titles of dozens of his more than four hundred published stories, and every guest receives a free copy of an O. Henry reader. His portrait hangs in the lobby. In it, he's at a desk leaning back in a leather chair, a plump man in a dark suit, red-cheeked, looking up from the newspaper he's reading, but with the faraway look of a man thinking about that bottle of gin in his bottom desk drawer. In 1910 he died of cirrhosis of the liver, diabetes, and an enlarged heart. He was forty-eight years old, the same age William was when he died.

I was introduced to the hotel, and to Dennis and Nancy, by the writer Wiley Cash, in 2016. Since then, they've allowed me to come whenever I've needed the space and time, a writing retreat for two or three day-long stretches. Space and time are among the essential not-so-secret ingredients necessary for writing, but especially for a story like this one. Without the O. Henry Hotel this book would not exist. Thank you.

All I learned through the research and composition of this book was filtered through my experience and point of view. Over time memories fade, but to the best of my knowledge everything in this book is true. However, the interpretations and conclusions are mine alone.

Kiss goodbye.